AF528223

THE ART OF ESCALATION

NAVIGATING COURAGE AND CLARITY IN THE MODERN WORKPLACE

astitva prakashan

THE ART OF ESCALATION

NAVIGATING COURAGE AND CLARITY IN THE MODERN WORKPLACE

SAURABH BHUTANI

Copyright © 2025 Saurabh Bhutani
All rights reserved.

No part of this publication may be reproduced, distributed, or transmitted in any form or by any means, electronic, mechanical, photocopying, recording, or otherwise, without the prior written permission of the author, except in the case of brief quotations used in critical reviews and articles.

For permissions, inquiries, and other correspondence, please contact:
asap.saurabhbhutani@gmail.com

ISBN: 978-93-344-5696-7

First Edition

This book is a work of nonfiction. While every effort has been made to ensure the accuracy and reliability of the information provided, the author and publisher assume no responsibility for errors or omissions. The views expressed are those of the author and do not constitute legal, financial, or organizational advice.

Acknowledgments

This book began as a reflection on a recurring theme in my professional life, why some issues find resolution, while others find resistance.

But as I wrote, it became something more: a tribute to the people, mentors, and colleagues who, knowingly or not, taught me the art of escalation through their own courage, restraint, and empathy.

Across my two decades of professional journey, I've had the privilege of working with teams that challenged my assumptions, leaders who trusted me to act with judgment, and mentors who taught me that silence can be strength, but only when it's chosen, not imposed.

To every colleague who ever asked, *"Should we escalate this?"* — thank you.

Each of those conversations shaped my understanding of not just when to speak, but how to speak.

This book is built on those everyday questions that define how modern organizations breathe and grow.

I owe deep gratitude to the leaders who led by example, those who didn't just teach process but modelled presence. To those who welcomed uncomfortable truths without defensiveness, who believed that escalation, when done right, is not a threat to hierarchy but a reflection of trust. Your authenticity continues to guide how I view leadership.

To my teams, past and present — thank you for your resilience and honesty.

You reminded me that escalation is not a skill confined to meeting rooms; it is a culture sustained by shared ownership.

Each late-night discussion, every thoughtful debate, and even moments of silence became part of the rhythm that led to this book.

To my mentors and peers in the professional ecosystem — thank you for holding the mirror up when I needed it most. Your questions sharpened my thinking; your stories enriched these pages.

And to those who disagreed constructively — your dissent kept this book honest.

My heartfelt appreciation goes to my family, whose patience and encouragement turned long hours of reflection into something meaningful.

You reminded me that clarity at work begins with calm at home.
Every page of this book carries traces of your support.

Finally, this book is also a note of gratitude to the corporate community itself — the vast, dynamic ecosystem where human behaviour meets ambition, deadlines, and purpose. It's where escalation unfolds daily in subtle, unseen ways through an email, a hesitation, a question asked at the right time.
This book belongs as much to those moments as it does to these words.

To everyone who ever chose courage over comfort, empathy over ego, and truth over silence — this book is for you.

Preface

*"Leadership is not the absence of conflict —
it is the ability to navigate it with clarity."*

In every corporate corridor, escalation is both feared and misunderstood.
It's that moment when an issue refuses to stay buried under emails, status reports, or polite silence.
It's when the choice to speak up begins to feel heavier than the comfort of staying quiet.

For years, I viewed escalation as an operational tool, a mechanism of communication in complex hierarchies.
It seemed procedural: gather facts, present evidence, and move the issue upward.
But experience, especially the kind earned through late-night calls, tense reviews, and difficult conversations taught me that **escalation is not a process; it's a pulse.**

It reflects how healthy a culture truly is, whether people can raise concerns without fear, and whether leaders can receive them without ego.

The Evolution: From Evidence to Empathy

In the early stages of my career, escalation meant *proof*. If you had the data, the documentation, the evidence, you had a case.
And while that foundation remains essential, I gradually realized that **facts alone don't move organizations forward, people do.** And people don't always respond to logic; they respond to trust.

The art of escalation, I learned, lies not in *proving a point*, but in *preserving a relationship while pursuing resolution.*
It is not about authority; it is about authenticity.

That shift, from evidence to empathy became the central theme of this book. Because in the modern workplace, escalation is no longer a one-dimensional act of reporting up. It's a multidimensional act of *bridging perspectives.* It demands courage to challenge, but also humility to connect.

Empathy does not replace evidence, it completes it.
It ensures that escalation builds trust, not tension.

Why This Book Exists

Over more than two decades of professional experience, across geographies, reporting lines, and leadership teams, I witnessed one constant truth:

Escalation defines character.

How a person escalates or chooses not to, reveals more about their judgment than their résumé ever will. The confident professional doesn't escalate to blame; they escalate to clarify. The insecure one escalates to shield. And the wise one escalates to improve the system, not to expose its cracks.

This book was born from those observations, the subtle art that separates the responsible voice from the reactive one. Because while escalation is a skill, **the art of escalation is a mindset.**

The Frameworks: CFIA and CIAE+

Through countless conversations, escalations, and reflections across my career, two frameworks slowly took shape, CFIA and CIAE+, each capturing a different facet of how leaders think and communicate under pressure.

The first, **CFIA — Clarify, Frame, Inform, Act**, became the *decision lens.*
It is a simple, structured way of thinking that helps leaders pause, analyse, and act with composure.
Before escalating, you must clarify the issue, frame it objectively, inform the right people, and act decisively.
CFIA ensures that escalation is not impulsive but intentional, driven by clarity, not emotion.

The second, **CIAE+ — Context, Impact, Ask, Evidence, Empathy**, became the *communication lens.*

It offers a practical way to express escalation, assertively yet respectfully.
Every effective message begins with context, conveys impact, clarifies the ask with evidence, and closes with empathy. CIAE+ ensures that what you say is not only heard, but received with understanding.

Together, CFIA and CIAE+ are not "models" in the textbook sense, they are **mindsets**.
They help leaders approach every difficult conversation with balance: structure from CFIA, and sincerity from CIAE+. In them lies a philosophy that escalation is neither about silence nor about noise, it's about **signal**.

The Human Side of Escalation

Through stories and scenarios in this book, you'll meet familiar characters:
the silent performer who avoids escalation until burnout sets in;
the eager escalator who confuses urgency with anxiety; and the seasoned leader who knows when not to escalate, because sometimes, restraint is the real mark of maturity.

These are not abstract profiles; they are people we work with, and sometimes, people we are.
Their stories remind us that escalation is not a skill to be perfected; it's a *temperament to be cultivated.*

Every chapter in this book blends logic with lived experience, frameworks with human nuance.
You'll find stories from boardrooms, cross-functional teams, and moments of silence that spoke louder than confrontation.
You'll also find reflections drawn from philosophy and leadership, because escalation, like wisdom, is both emotional and ethical.

Escalation with Empathy

At its heart, this book is a manifesto for **Escalation with Empathy**.
Because the future of leadership isn't about knowing how to speak louder, it's about knowing how to speak *right.*
Escalation with empathy means telling difficult truths without hostility, confronting hierarchy without fear, and resolving conflict without burning bridges.

It is what transforms an individual contributor into a leader — someone who doesn't just identify problems, but stewards solutions.

Escalation with empathy is the art of combining courage with consideration.
It's the discipline of saying what needs to be said, in a way others can hear.

This book is not a manual, it's a mirror.
It invites you to reflect on how you show up when stakes rise. Because the ultimate measure of professional maturity isn't whether you escalate, it's **how you do it**.

If this book succeeds in helping you pause before pressing "send," listen before reacting, and choose courage tempered with clarity — then its purpose is fulfilled.

Escalation, when done with empathy, doesn't divide, it defines.
It builds trust, strengthens systems, and turns discomfort into growth.

Author's Note

"I didn't write this book to teach escalation —
I wrote it to understand it."

This book was born not out of theory, but out of observation, drawn from the meeting rooms, project reviews, and everyday corporate crossroads where people wrestle with the same question: *"Should I escalate this?"*
Over more than two decades, I found that this question never truly leaves the workplace, it simply changes shape. Sometimes it's an internal conflict: whether to speak up. Sometimes it's relational: how to raise something without damaging trust.

And sometimes it's organizational: how to create a culture where escalation isn't feared, but valued.

The Art of Escalation grew from these reflections, from moments where I stayed silent when I should have spoken, and others where I spoke too soon and learned the cost of timing.

In between those experiences lay the insight that escalation is not about **who's right**, but **what's right**.

It's not about power, it's about **principle**.

Over time, I came to see escalation as a discipline that sits at the intersection of three forces: **clarity, courage, and empathy**.

Clarity to know what truly matters.

Courage to act when silence feels safer.

And empathy to do both without alienating those around you.

That belief shaped the twin frameworks at the heart of this book — **CFIA** and **CIAE+**.

They are not checklists but companions for thoughtful leadership:

- **CFIA — Clarify, Frame, Inform, Act** — is a *decision lens.* It helps you pause and think before you act.
- **CIAE+ — Context, Impact, Ask, Evidence, Empathy** — is a *communication lens.* It guides you to speak in ways that influence without inflaming.

Together, they form the anatomy of escalation done right, where structure meets sincerity.

But beneath every model and reflection in these pages lies a simpler truth: escalation is deeply human.

It tests judgment, patience, and composure more than it tests skill.
And it often mirrors who we are under pressure, not what our roles demand, but what our values allow.

This book is an invitation, not to escalate more, but to **escalate better**.
To see escalation not as confrontation, but as contribution.
To approach difficult conversations not with the intent to prove, but to improve.
And to recognize that in today's workplaces, *how we escalate* defines *how we lead.*

If even one reader closes this book with the confidence to speak truth with empathy, to turn discomfort into dialogue, then this journey will have been worth it.

Because in the end, escalation isn't about hierarchy or process flow. It's about **raising what matters, responsibly.**

— *Saurabh Bhutani*
New Delhi, India

CONTENTS

Chapter 1 : What is Escalation? 1

Chapter 2 : The Anatomy and Psychology of Escalation 8

Chapter 3 : The Cost of Poor Escalation 16

Chapter 4 : The Escalation Toolkit 22

Chapter 5 : The Golden Rules of Escalation 31

Chapter 6 : Escalation in Matrix Organizations 37

Chapter 7 : Escalation in Crises / High-Stakes Situations..... 42

Chapter 8 : Escalation Templates and Scripts 47

Chapter 9 : Escalating Up Without Backlash 56

Chapter 10 : Escalation Across Cultures (Global Contexts). 62

Chapter 11 : Digital Escalations (Escalating in the Age of Remote Work & AI) 69

Chapter 12 : De-escalation as a Skill 76

Chapter 13 : The Escalation Playbook for Leaders 82

Chapter 14 ; Stories from the Trenches 89

Chapter 15 : The Future of Escalation —AI, Ethics, and Beyond 98

Chapter 16 : What We've Learned —The Discipline Behind Courage 104

Epilogue : Escalate to Elevate 112

Sources/References 113

CHAPTER 1

WHAT IS ESCALATION?

> ***“"If you never escalate, you’re invisible. If you escalate everything, you're intolerable. The art is in knowing when and how."***

Escalation is not about raising alarms — it’s about raising awareness. In corporate settings, escalation means bringing a critical issue to someone with the authority or perspective to resolve it. It's a sign of ownership, not failure.

Escalation is a form of **professional courage** when done right.

> ***“Escalation done right is not confrontation, but clarity in motion.” – Anonymous***

Escalation is one of the most misunderstood practices in corporate life. Many see it as a negative act, a sign of weakness, or even betrayal. In truth, escalation is a disciplined process of ensuring that the right problem is visible at the right level so it can be solved.

Defining Escalation

In a corporate context, escalation can be defined as: **“The conscious act of transferring decision-making or problem ownership up the chain of command or across**

functions when a resolution cannot be reached at the current level."

This is not about **complaining** or **blame-shifting**. Rather, it's about structured communication.

- **Reporting** = Providing updates on progress.
- **Complaining** = Venting frustration without solutions.
- **Whistleblowing** = Escalating violations or ethical breaches outside normal channels.
- **Escalation** = Ensuring visibility of a critical issue to the right decision-makers.

Escalation is how organizations shift problems to a new level of thinking.

Common Misconceptions

Employees often hesitate because of three myths:

1. *"Escalating makes me look weak."*
2. *"My boss will think I can't handle it."*
3. *"Escalation will burn relationships."*

In fact, effective escalation shows **ownership, courage, and foresight.**

"Management is doing things right; leadership is doing the right things."
– Peter Drucker
Escalation, when appropriate, is leadership in action.

Why Escalation is Necessary

No matter how competent a team is, there will always be:

- **Conflicts of interest** (priorities differ across functions).
- **Resource bottlenecks** (not enough people, money, or time).
- **Authority gaps** (decisions beyond your pay grade).

Without escalation, problems linger, projects slip, and organizations bleed efficiency.
With escalation, issues are exposed and resolved faster — sometimes saving reputations, revenue, or careers.

"An ounce of prevention is worth a pound of cure."
– Benjamin Franklin
Escalation is prevention in practice.

---

4. Escalation as Professional Courage

Escalation is not a sign of failure but of **professional maturity.**
It requires judgment, timing, and emotional control.

Picture a Monday morning project review. PowerPoints are polished, timelines are "green" on the RAG status, but the body language around the table tells another story. Deadlines have already slipped, dependencies remain unresolved, and nobody wants to be the first to "escalate." Everyone hopes someone else will raise the red flag. The silence is deafening.

This is the **corporate paradox**: escalation is discouraged culturally ("don't bypass your manager") yet punished when absent ("why didn't you raise this earlier?").

"You cannot solve a problem with the same level of thinking that created it." – Albert Einstein

---

Defining Escalation in the Corporate Reality

Escalation is more than transferring a problem upwards. It is a **social contract** within the organization:

- You admit a problem exists.
- You demonstrate ownership by making it visible.
- You trust leadership to act.

But culture often complicates this. In **hierarchical organizations**, escalation is seen as challenging authority. In **flat organizations**, escalation risks being labelled as "not being collaborative enough."

In multinationals, an escalation email often reads like a press release — carefully worded, CC'd across continents, with phrases like *"for visibility"* and *"for alignment"* softening the blow.

Myths & Mindsets

- *The Hero Myth:* Believing that solving everything alone shows strength.

- *The Loyalty Myth:* Thinking escalation equals disloyalty to your immediate boss.
- *The Harmony Myth:* Believing that avoiding escalation preserves team culture.

Reality: these myths delay resolution and magnify damage.

Escalation vs. Other Corporate Behaviours

- **Reporting** → *Routine, factual updates.*
- **Complaining** → *Emotion-laden, blame-heavy venting.*
- **Whistleblowing** → *Ethical/legal breaches reported through formal channels.*
- **Escalation** → *Focused, timely surfacing of issues to unblock progress.*

Escalation is the corporate equivalent of pulling the emergency brake, not because you dislike the train, but because you want to save it from derailment.

The Courage to Escalate

In cultures obsessed with "self-sufficiency," escalation is countercultural. It requires **corporate courage**: the ability to accept that visibility may bring scrutiny, but silence will bring failure.

"Courage is not the absence of fear, but rather the judgment that something else is more important than fear." – Ambrose Redmoon

---

Closing Thought

Escalation is neither an act of defiance nor a sign of failure. It is an act of responsibility — a deliberate choice to bring visibility, context, and urgency to an issue that cannot, and should not, be resolved in isolation. It demands judgment, not impulsiveness, conviction, not confrontation.

In its truest form, escalation is an expression of care — for the outcome, for the team, and for the integrity of the process. When done well, it builds trust and accelerates clarity; when mishandled, it breeds defensiveness and division. The difference lies not in the hierarchy of who escalates to whom, but in the *intent* behind the act, whether it is to illuminate or to implicate.

Every organization, regardless of size or culture, eventually reveals its own philosophy of escalation. Some treat it as a tool of accountability, others as a taboo of confrontation. Yet, the healthiest cultures are those that normalize escalation as part of collective intelligence, where speaking up is not seen as dissent, but as contribution.

As we step into the next chapter, we begin to explore the inner anatomy of this act, the psychological wiring that determines *when* and *why* individuals choose to escalate or remain silent. For at the heart of every escalation lies a human instinct — to be heard, to be understood, and to do what's right.

Escalation is the paradoxical skill:

- Too much, and you're branded disruptive.
- Too little, and you're branded negligent.

The mastery lies in being the person who escalates with precision, not the loudest voice, but the clearest signal.

> ***"The single biggest problem in communication is the illusion that it has taken place." – George Bernard Shaw***

Chapter 2

The Anatomy and Psychology of Escalation

> ***"He who knows others is wise; he who knows himself is enlightened." – Lao Tzu***

Escalation combines rational and emotional triggers. Rationally, it is about resource bottlenecks, missed deadlines, or misaligned priorities. Psychologically, it is about frustration, power dynamics, and the innate human tendency to be heard. Understanding both dimensions is crucial for deciding when to act.

The Psychology Behind Escalation

It's 9:45 PM, and you're staring at a draft escalation email. You've rewritten the subject line six times. *"Escalation: Critical Delay"* sounds too harsh. *"Update: Risk to Timeline"* feels too soft. You hover over the CC line — should you copy your boss's boss?

This is the psychology of escalation: a battle between rational need (unblock the issue) and emotional fear (don't get branded as a troublemaker).

---

1. Fear as the First Barrier

Escalation triggers **corporate anxiety**:

- Will my manager think I can't handle this?
- Will my peers see me as undermining them?
- Will leadership question why I waited this long?

The result is often paralysis — *inaction disguised as "waiting for the right time."*

---

2. Personality Types in Escalation

- **The Avoider** → Keeps issues under wraps until they explode in Quarterly Business Reviews.
- **The Firefighter** → Raises alarms daily, eroding credibility.
- **The Diplomat** → Escalates after private conversations, framing it as collective risk.
- **The Opportunist** → Uses escalation to spotlight others' failures.
- **The Strategist** → Escalates with data, context, and timing trusted even when the message is hard.

"Reputation is like fine China once broken, it's very difficult to repair."
– Abraham Lincoln
Choose your escalation style carefully.

---

3. Emotional Intelligence in Escalation

Corporate Emotional Quotient means:

- **Self-awareness:** Recognizing if you're escalating out of frustration or genuine risk.
- **Empathy:** Considering how the recipient will *feel* when they read the message.
- **Social awareness:** Reading the unspoken — sometimes an escalation is less about the content and more about *who delivers it to whom.*
- **Self-regulation:** Choosing calm, neutral language that invites collaboration.

Example:

❌ *"This delay is unacceptable."*

☑ *"We risk missing delivery unless the resource gap is addressed. Can leadership help resolve?"*

---

4. Neuroscience & the Threat Response

Escalation feels threatening because it touches the **SCARF model** (David Rock):

- Status (fear of looking weak)
- Certainty (not knowing the outcome)
- Autonomy (loss of control)
- Relatedness (risking team harmony)
- Fairness (fear of being blamed disproportionately)

This is why many escalation emails start with disclaimers like *"This is not about blame, but about ensuring delivery risk is visible."*

---

5. Escalation as Leadership Maturity

Counterintuitively, those who escalate responsibly build trust. Leaders remember the person who raised the flag before the ship hit the iceberg.

"Leadership is about making others better as a result of your presence and making sure that impact lasts in your absence." – Sheryl Sandberg

Escalation is one of the subtle ways rising leaders show they can balance courage with tact.

Escalation is both **a human act of vulnerability** and **a professional act of leadership.** The best leaders are those who mastered the psychology of *when, how, and why* to escalate.

In corporate life, silence is rarely neutral. Either it protects harmony, or it conceals disaster.

The Anatomy of Escalation

"What gets measured gets managed — but what gets escalated gets resolved." — Inspired by Peter Drucker

Escalation is not a single event. It is a structured process, and like all processes, it has anatomy.

1. **Trigger Point** – The moment you recognize the issue cannot be resolved at your level. It could be a

resource crunch, a compliance breach, a budget overrun, or simply a decision stuck in organizational gridlock.

2. **Framing the Issue** – Escalation is not just about *raising a hand*; it's about *framing the problem.* Who is affected? What is the impact? What has been tried? Without clarity, escalation is noise.

3. **Choosing the Path** – Do you escalate vertically (up the chain of command), laterally (to a peer function), or diagonally (to a governance body or steering committee)? Each path has different political consequences.

4. **Timing and Data** – Escalating without data is speculation. Escalating too late is negligence. Leaders respect foresight — not hindsight.

5. **Closure Loop** – The true anatomy of escalation includes closing the loop. Once the issue is addressed, document what worked, what didn't, and how to prevent recurrence.

In corporate culture, escalation is often judged not by the content of the message but by the *craft of delivery.* A poorly worded escalation email can make you look accusatory. A well-framed one makes you look accountable.

Think of escalation not as pulling an alarm bell but as drafting a **case file** — evidence, context, and a clear request for action.

Escalation psychology is where fear, ego, trust, and culture collide.

- **Fear:** Employees hesitate to escalate because they fear being judged incapable.
- **Ego:** Managers resist escalations because they see them as a slight to their authority.
- **Trust:** The same message, delivered by a credible employee versus one perceived as political, will land very differently.

In many organizations, escalation is less about facts and more about perception.

The Culture of Silence

In hierarchical firms, employees often suffer in silence, hoping the problem will solve itself. But silence is expensive. Delayed escalation has sunk billion-dollar deals, missed regulatory deadlines, and caused irreparable reputational damage.

Escalation, in such cultures, becomes not just a management skill but an act of cultural courage.

When Escalation Fails vs. Succeeds

Case 1: The Project That Nearly Sank

Arjun, a project manager, avoided escalating an integration failure for fear of looking weak. Six months later, the issue blew up in the boardroom. The client walked away. Millions were lost.

Lesson: Not escalating was the bigger weakness.

Case 2: The Transparent Leader

Meera, another leader, spotted a regulatory risk early. She escalated immediately, with data in hand. The CFO intervened, the issue was resolved, and the client praised the firm's transparency.

Lesson: Escalation, when framed with foresight, builds trust.

Closing Thought

Escalation, at its core, is not a procedural act — it is a deeply human one. It sits at the crossroads of personality, perception, and purpose. Different personality types approach it in distinctly different ways: the assertive personalities see escalation as a means of accountability; the analytical ones wait for all data before acting; the amiable types hesitate, fearing disruption to harmony; while the expressive ones may over-communicate, hoping to be heard through volume rather than clarity. Each brings its own strength and shadow.

Yet beneath these differences lies a universal undercurrent — *fear*. Fear of judgment, of damaging relationships, of being perceived as incapable or confrontational. This fear, when unaddressed, often silences escalation before it begins. And it is here that **emotional intelligence** plays its quiet but decisive role. The ability to recognize one's emotions, regulate them, and read the emotions of others turns escalation from a reactive impulse into a calibrated response.

When leaders use empathy to frame facts, when they can sense both the heat and the heartbeat of a situation, escalation becomes not a breaking point but a bridge. The mastery of escalation, therefore, does not lie in one's title or temperament but in one's ability to combine awareness with action, and emotion with ethics. That is the true anatomy of escalation, a blend of logic and empathy, fear, and courage, which leads not just to resolution, but to trust.

Escalation psychology is the psychology of timing and trust. Those who master it are not seen as managers of crises but as leaders of foresight.

"Escalation is not betrayal; it is stewardship." — Anonymous

"Escalation begins in the mind before it moves to the mouth." – Corporate Proverb

---

Chapter 3
The Cost of Poor Escalation

> ***"The most important thing in communication is hearing what isn't said." – Peter Drucker***

In corporate world, silence can be more dangerous than words. Leaders often avoid escalating sensitive issues to protect reputations, but silence can allow problems to fester. Escalation here requires courage, tact, and timing.

Friday evening. The project dashboard still shows everything in "green." Yet, deep down, everyone knows a critical vendor delivery hasn't even left the factory floor. No one wants to escalate, not the vendor manager (who doesn't want to look incompetent), not the project lead (who promised the deadline in last month's steering committee), and certainly not the junior analyst (who's already been told "don't create panic").

By Monday, the delay is visible to everyone, including the client.
The escalation has now happened — but not on your terms.

---

1. The Hidden Costs of Delay

The first and most obvious consequence of poor escalation is **time lost.**

- **Projects slip:** A 2-day delay ignored often snowballs into a 2-week crisis.
- **Reactive firefighting:** Leaders spend more energy explaining delays than fixing them.
- **Lost trust:** Stakeholders begin to assume that every "green" dashboard hides a "red" reality.

"A stitch in time saves nine." – Proverb
Escalation is that first stitch; without it, the tear only widens.

---

2. Case Study A: The Silent Deadline

A global IT services company promised a major bank a system migration in 90 days. Midway, the technical team realized the vendor's software patch was incompatible. Instead of escalating, they tried to "work around" it. By Day 75, they had no working solution.

- Result: Project delayed by 4 months.
- Cost: $12M in penalties and a dented client relationship.
- Internal fallout: The project manager was moved out, and the team's morale plummeted.

Lesson: Escalating at Day 30 would have brought leadership intervention, new vendor negotiations, and a realistic reset. Silence cost credibility.

---

3. The Political Cost of Escalation Avoidance

In many organizations, not escalating is seen as "protecting harmony." But harmony built on silence is fragile.

- **Boss Shock:** Leaders hate surprises. Nothing erodes trust faster than walking into a steering committee unprepared for a red status update.
- **Peer Resentment:** Colleagues begin to see you as unreliable, the one who hides problems until they explode.
- **Career Stagnation:** Ironically, avoiding escalation to "look good" often makes you invisible.

Escalation avoidance is reputation erosion.

"You can't build a reputation on what you are going to do." – Henry Ford

---

4. Case Study B: The Cultural Trap

In a large Asian conglomerate, the unwritten rule was *"never escalate above your immediate manager."* A supply chain lead discovered a major vendor was near bankruptcy. Instead of escalating beyond his boss, he kept quiet. His boss, fearing loss of face, also stayed quiet.

By the time the CFO found out, the vendor had collapsed, leaving the company with stranded shipments worth millions.

Lesson: Corporate culture that discourages escalation creates systemic blindness. The cost is borne by everyone.

---

5. The Personal Cost

Failure to escalate doesn't just harm projects — it harms people.

- Employees carry **hidden stress** of unresolved issues.
- "Escalation guilt" eats away at confidence — *"If I had spoken up earlier, could this have been avoided?"*
- Careers stall because silence is mistaken for incompetence, not loyalty.

Failing to escalate ensures you hit that ceiling faster.

---

6. Escalation at the Wrong Time

Ironically, poor escalation isn't just silence — it's also noise at the wrong time.

- **Too early:** Escalating before attempting solutions makes you look incapable.
- **Too late:** Escalating when damage is already visible makes you look negligent.
- **Too loud:** Copying half the organization creates politics instead of solutions.

Corporate nuance: This is why "escalation etiquette" exists in seasoned organizations. Leaders ask not just *"what was escalated?"* but *"when and how?"*

Closing Thought

Every case we have seen in this chapter, whether it was the quiet crisis that unfolded in the boardroom, the delayed decision that cost a client relationship, or the team that mistook silence for alignment reveals a common thread: the absence of timely and responsible escalation.

The true cost of poor escalation is rarely measured in financial terms alone. It is felt in eroded trust, in lost credibility, in the unspoken fatigue that seeps into teams when issues linger unresolved. Projects falter not just because of poor strategy, but because of misplaced politeness. Leaders lose influence not because they lack vision, but because they misjudge the moment to act. And organizations lose agility when culture confuses harmony with avoidance.

Poor escalation does not announce itself with noise; it creeps in through hesitation. It thrives in environments where fear outweighs transparency and where communication is mistaken for compliance.

Yet, as each case study also shows, the story does not have to end in loss. Every misstep carries a mirror, a reminder that escalation, when approached with courage and context, can restore alignment faster than any post-crisis analysis ever could.

The question, then, is not whether escalation is costly — it is whether *silence costs more.*

In the next chapter, we move from reflection to action — exploring the tools, frameworks, and signals that can help professionals decide *when to escalate, what to escalate,* and *how to do it right.* For it is only through structure and self-awareness that escalation becomes not a reaction, but a rhythm.

Poor escalation has three costs:

- To the **organization** (missed deadlines, financial losses).
- To the **team** (stress, resentment, blame games).
- To the **individual** (trust lost, credibility questioned).

Escalation is inevitable. The only question is: will you do it on your terms, or will the situation escalate itself on its own terms?

> ***"Silence can escalate faster than words." – Anonymous***

CHAPTER 4
THE ESCALATION TOOLKIT

"Give me six hours to chop down a tree and I will spend the first four sharpening the axe." – Abraham Lincoln

When to escalate, whom to escalate to, what to escalate, and how to escalate. Timing, tone, and medium often matter as much as the facts themselves.

Escalation Mastery — Real-World Playbook

"Mastery is not knowing more, it's knowing exactly when and how to act." — Corporate Maxim

By now, you understand **what escalation is, why it matters, the psychology behind it, when to escalate, and how to do it effectively**. Let's move to a **practical playbook** — the kind of guidance you can use in the heat of corporate life.

---

1. The 5-Step Escalation Framework

Every escalation should follow a structured approach:

Step 1: Identify the Issue

- Ask yourself: *"Is this issue critical to delivery, compliance, reputation, or financial outcomes?"*

- Consider scope: Is it local (team-level) or strategic (cross-functional or organizational)?

Tip: Keep a **risk log**. Issues that appear in multiple areas often justify escalation sooner rather than later.

Step 2: Prepare the Facts

- Quantify the impact: cost, timeline, and resource implications.
- Document prior actions and attempted solutions.
- Map dependencies: which teams, clients, or vendors are affected?
- Suggest potential actions — even partial solutions show ownership.

Corporate nuance: In multinational firms, include **time-zone-adjusted deadlines** or **local regulatory context**.

Step 3: Choose the Right Channel

- **Vertical:** When authority or budget approval is needed.
- **Lateral:** To collaborate with peer functions.
- **Diagonal:** Committees or governance boards for strategic cross-functional risks.

Tip: For global teams, adapt the approach to local culture. In hierarchical Asian teams, align with your manager first. In

Western teams, a direct, evidence-based escalation may be preferred.

Step 4: Frame the Message

Use the **C-I-A-E formula**:

1. **Context** – What's happening?
2. **Impact** – What's at risk if unaddressed?
3. **Ask for the Action Required** – What decisions or approvals are needed?
4. **Evidence** – Attach data, charts, emails, or screenshots.

Sample Boardroom-Ready Email:

Subject: Escalation: Risk of Delivery Delay – Project Phoenix

Body:
Context: Module X cannot integrate with legacy system Y.
Impact: 3-week delay; potential $500K overrun; SLA at risk.
Action Required: Approve vendor support & contingency resources.
Evidence: Logs, test results, prior correspondence attached.

Step 5: Close the Loop

- Confirm actions taken by leadership.
- Update all stakeholders.
- Document lessons for future escalations.

Corporate nuance: Following up consistently builds credibility and shows your escalation was **strategic, not reactive**.

Escalation doesn't begin when you write an email — it begins when you *think*. That is why, let's look at a framework that helps you **decide** how to escalate, not just *execute* it.

That framework is the **C-F-I-A model** — the *decision lens.*

CFIA = Clarify → Frame → Inform → Act

If the 5-Step Escalation Process tells you *what to do,* **CFIA tells you *how to think before you do it.***

The CFIA Model — Thinking Before Acting

- **Clarify — What is the real issue?**

This is the mental pause leaders take before reacting. Clarify the facts, separate emotion from pattern, and identify what is truly blocking progress.

Escalation maturity begins with self-awareness.

- **Frame — How do I structure the issue?**

Frame the issue in a way that is objective, relevant, and aligned to the listener's context.
A well-framed escalation builds alignment; a messy one breeds defensiveness.

If you frame it well, half the conflict dissolves.

- ❖ **Inform — Who needs to know and why?**

Not everyone needs the same information.
Inform the right stakeholders with transparency and precision.

Inform builds trust. Over-inform creates noise.

- ❖ **Act — What is the appropriate next step?**

Once clarity and framing are complete, action becomes natural.
Act could mean:

- resolve at your level,
- escalate upward,
- align sideways,
- or pause briefly while new information arrives.

Action completes clarity.

---

2. Escalation Etiquette: The Subtle Rules

- **Avoid panic language:** "Urgent" or "Critical" should be used sparingly.
- **Limit CCs:** Only include stakeholders who need visibility; too many leads to confusion.
- **Maintain neutrality:** Focus on facts, not blame.
- **Escalate once per issue:** Repetition erodes trust.

- **Prioritize solutions:** Leaders value escalations framed with **proposed actions**.

---

3. Boardroom Scenarios: Applied Mastery

Scenario A: Resource Shortage

- **Issue:** Key resource unavailable for critical client deliverable.
- **Escalation:** Email to VP of Operations + conversation with HR manager.
- **Outcome:** Resource reallocation approved within 24 hours; project stays on track.

Scenario B: Compliance Risk

- **Issue:** Missing regulatory input on a filing.
- **Escalation:** Escalation call to CFO and Legal Head, supported with risk assessment.
- **Outcome:** Immediate corrective action; leadership praises proactive visibility.

Scenario C: Cross-Functional Conflict

- **Issue:** Design and Development teams disagree on technical approach.
- **Escalation:** Meeting escalated to CTO with both team leads; data-driven comparison prepared.
- **Outcome:** CTO decides on the solution; teams align without blame.

---

4. Common Mistakes to Avoid

Mistake	Consequence	Correction
Escalating too early	Perceived incompetence	Attempt local solutions first
Escalating too late	Missed deadlines, reputational loss	Monitor triggers and act before crisis
Over-escalation	Credibility erosion	Prioritize issues with strategic impact
Poorly framed message	Misinterpretation, delays	Use C-I-A-E structure
Emotional escalation	Political backlash	Maintain neutral, professional tone

---

5. Building Escalation Confidence

- Keep a **personal escalation journal** — track what worked, what didn't.
- Practice **mini-escalations** for low-risk issues to build confidence.
- Seek mentorship: leaders who value escalation can coach timing, framing, and channels.

Closing Thought

"Confidence in escalation comes from preparation, experience, and understanding your organizational culture."

In this chapter, we dissected the mechanics of escalation — *when* to escalate, *whom* to escalate to, *what* to escalate, and *how* to deliver it with precision and purpose. We learned that effective escalation is not an act of hierarchy, but an act of stewardship — the responsibility to ensure issues find the right visibility at the right time.

The toolkit we explored, from identifying early warning signs and stakeholder mapping to balancing facts with tone and timing — is not a checklist to be followed blindly. It is a compass, not a calendar. Each situation demands discernment: what may call for escalation in one context might require restraint in another.

The greatest value of the toolkit lies not in its structure but in its **intent**. Tools serve only when anchored in integrity. Templates and frameworks help professionals navigate complexity, but wisdom lies in reading the nuances, in knowing when to step forward and when to allow space for self-resolution.

As we move ahead, the next chapter distils these insights into a set of timeless behavioural principles — the **Golden Rules of Escalation**. Because while tools give us methods, it is rules that give us meaning. Together, they turn escalation from a process into a practice, one grounded not just in efficiency, but in ethics.

Escalation mastery is not just about moving problems upward; it is **a leadership skill**. It demonstrates foresight, judgment, and accountability. The professional who can escalate **strategically, factually, and culturally astutely** becomes indispensable, not because they complain, but because they prevent crises before they escalate on their own.

"Mastering escalation is mastering influence without authority."

"Tools don't solve problems; they guide humans to solutions." – Anonymous

---

Evolution of the CIAE Framework

"Frameworks evolve, just as leaders do."

When the **CIAE framework** was first introduced in this chapter, the "E" stood for **Evidence** — emphasizing the need for facts, documentation, and data to support an escalation. That foundation remains vital, as credibility begins with truth.

Yet, as this book progresses, the framework matures. The "E" expands to mean **Empathy** — recognizing that facts alone rarely resolve conflict; relationships do.

Empathy does not replace evidence; it completes it. It reframes escalation from a transactional act into a human one, where understanding is valued as much as accuracy.

Evidence convinces the mind; empathy moves the heart. Together, they make escalation truly effective.

CHAPTER 5
THE GOLDEN RULES OF ESCALATION

"Rules are not necessarily sacred, principles are." – Franklin D. Roosevelt

Rule #1: Escalate facts, not frustration. Rule #2: Escalate up, not around. Rule #3: Allow a chance for self-resolution first. Rule #4: Document, document, document. These rules ensure escalation remains a constructive process.

"Knowing when to escalate is as important as knowing when to remain silent." — Corporate Maxim

Escalation is a powerful tool, but like any tool, misuse can cause harm. Over-escalation, premature escalation, or escalation without preparation can erode credibility, strain relationships, and create unnecessary organizational noise.

The key is **judgment**, rooted in understanding the *problem, the audience, and the context.*

1. The Cost of Over-Escalation

In many organizations, certain employees escalate every minor hiccup. The result?

- **Credibility erosion:** Leaders start ignoring alarms because "everything is urgent."
- **Frustration among peers:** Teams feel micromanaged or undermined.
- **Political backlash:** Repeated over-escalation may signal lack of confidence or attention to detail.

VP (exasperated): *"We don't need a daily email on every minor delay. Pick your battles."*

Team Lead (sheepish): *"I thought escalation was expected…"*
CEO (interjecting): *"Yes, but escalation is about impact, not visibility. Not every hiccup deserves the executive spotlight."*

In matrix organizations, over-escalation often triggers **'cc culture'** — where emails are copied across dozens of leaders, creating anxiety and distracting from real priorities.

---

2. When Escalation Is Premature

Escalation before thorough analysis can backfire:

- **Perceived incompetence:** "Why escalate before attempting solutions?"
- **Loss of trust:** Leaders may feel you are raising alarms without data.
- **Team disruption:** Jumping the chain can demoralize peers who were still troubleshooting.

Senior Manager: *"Why are you bringing this to me without validating with your team?"*
Junior Lead: *"I didn't want to wait…"*

Manager (calmly): *"Patience and preparation are part of escalation. Premature escalation signals panic, not ownership."*

---

3. Escalation Without Data

Escalation is persuasive only when backed by **facts, trends, and evidence**.

- Raising concerns with gut feeling alone may trigger defensive reactions.
- Leaders respect **structured escalation**: context, analysis, impact, and potential solutions.

Corporate nuance: This is why seasoned escalators often maintain a **mini "impact dossier"** — spreadsheets, risk charts, and annotated emails — so the escalation is impossible to misinterpret.

---

4. Escalation as a Political Tool

Using escalation to gain visibility or undermine colleagues is a fast track to damage:

- Peers feel mistrusted; collaboration suffers.
- Leadership sees the action as self-serving rather than problem-solving.
- The escalator's reputation as a team player diminishes.

Colleague whispers: *"She escalated the issue to the CFO just to show me up."*

CFO (to the team): *"Escalation is for resolution, not performance theatre."*

---

5. When to Hold Back

Escalation should be withheld when:

1. **The issue is minor** and can be resolved locally.
2. **Resolution is imminent** and raising it now adds noise.
3. **Escalation will cause disproportionate alarm** without tangible benefit.
4. **Cultural or political context dictates sensitivity** — for example, in highly hierarchical teams, going directly to a senior leader without alignment may backfire.

Knowing when to remain silent is not cowardice; it is strategic patience.

---

6. Balancing Escalation and Discretion

Great leaders instinctively ask:

- *What is the potential impact if I escalate?*
- *Will the audience understand and act, or be distracted?*
- *Do I have sufficient information to make the case?*

They escalate **strategically**, not habitually.

Often, informal channels, a coffee conversation with a mentor, a hallway check-in with a peer manager, or a pre-meeting alert can be more effective than formal escalation.

Closing Thought

The essence of escalation lies not in the process, but in the *principles* that govern it. The four golden rules we have explored — to escalate facts, not frustration; to escalate up, not around; to allow for self-resolution before intervention; and to document every step are more than procedural guidance. They are ethical anchors in a sea of ambiguity.

These rules remind us that escalation is as much about self-regulation as it is about communication. They compel us to pause before reacting, to replace assumption with evidence, and to channel urgency through respect. The real maturity of a professional is revealed not in the ability to escalate quickly, but in the discipline to escalate wisely.

When applied consistently, these principles reshape corporate culture. They encourage transparency without aggression, accountability without blame, and dialogue without defensiveness. They remind teams that escalation done right preserves dignity on both sides, it solves the issue without damaging the relationship.

Escalation is a double-edged sword. Done well, it prevents crises, builds trust, and signals leadership potential. Done poorly, it damages credibility, creates political friction, and erodes team morale.

"Silence at the wrong time is costly. Noise at the wrong time is destructive. Mastery lies in timing, discretion, and judgment."

As we move forward, we enter a more complex terrain — the **matrix organization**, where accountability is distributed, lines of reporting blur, and influence often outweighs authority. It is in this landscape that the true test of these rules begins. For in such environments, escalation ceases to be linear, it becomes strategic. And only those who understand both the tools and the ethics of escalation can navigate it successfully.

"Rules anchor escalation in fairness, not fury." – Corporate Wisdom

Chapter 6
Escalation in Matrix Organizations

"Structure should not be a straitjacket; it should be a framework for freedom." – Henry Mintzberg

Matrix organizations complicate escalation with dotted-line reporting and conflicting authority structures. Here, escalation requires political capital, cultural sensitivity, and clear communication across time zones.

"In a matrix, power is rarely absolute, it is distributed, negotiated, and often invisible." — Anonymous.

Matrix organizations are the modern corporate jungle gyms — dynamic, flexible, and highly political. They enable agility but also create confusion: dotted-line reporting, multiple bosses, cross-border teams, and decisions that need alignment across cultures and time zones.

In such structures, escalation becomes both **more critical and more delicate**. Who truly "owns" the problem? Who has the authority to fix it? And how do you escalate without offending one leader while informing another?

---

1. The Complexity of Dotted-Line Reporting

In a matrix, dotted lines create dual accountability. For employees, this means one manager signs the appraisal, while another dictates daily work.

- **Escalation challenge:** Which manager do you escalate to? The solid-line (formal authority) or the dotted-line (operational authority)?
- **Nuance:** Escalating to one without informing the other risks political fallout.

Employee: "I raised the vendor issue with my project sponsor."
Solid-line Manager: "Why didn't you bring it to me first?"
Employee: "Because you're not in the project loop."
Manager: "That's not the point, perception matters."

Lesson: In dotted-line environments, **parallel communication** is often safer than selective escalation.

---

2. Managing Global Teams Across Time Zones

When teams are spread across continents, escalation carries an additional burden — the **time lag**.

- A critical decision in New York may sit idle for 12 hours until Singapore wakes up.
- By then, the problem may have already escalated on its own.

Best practices:

- Use **asynchronous escalation channels** (escalation dashboards, trackers, documented updates).
- Always mark **time sensitivity** — "Action required within 24 hours" vs. "For awareness."
- Respect cultural norms — some cultures expect directness; others prefer softened escalation.

Example: A German Project Manager escalated bluntly to an American executive: "We are behind schedule because of repeated U.S. delays." While factually correct, the tone created defensiveness. A softer phrasing "We need stronger alignment across regions to meet shared timelines" would have preserved collaboration.

---

3. Political Capital and Influence Without Authority

Matrix organizations thrive on **influence over authority**. You may not have the title to command action, but you can still escalate effectively if you have **political capital**.

- Political capital comes from **credibility, networks, and past delivery.**
- Leaders listen more to those who have consistently demonstrated judgment and reliability.

Escalation in a matrix is less about hierarchy and more about **alliances**. A junior employee with credibility across regions may be heard more than a disengaged senior leader.

A regional lead in India needed urgent support from a European function. Instead of escalating formally, he leveraged relationships built in earlier projects to influence peers. When escalation did happen, it was **endorsed by multiple stakeholders** and carried more weight.

Closing Thought

"Power in a matrix is not about control, but about connection." — Rosabeth Moss Kanter

In a matrix organization, escalation is both an art and a negotiation. It is rarely about hierarchy, it is about influence. When authority is distributed and accountability is shared, the challenge is not *who* to escalate to, but *how* to do so without disrupting the delicate web of collaboration.

Throughout this chapter, we have seen how time zones, dotted-line reporting, and cultural diversity create both richness and friction. The same message, when interpreted through different lenses, can inspire trust or trigger defensiveness. This is why escalation in matrix structures demands not only clarity of facts, but also *emotional geometry* — the ability to read power, proximity, and perception in equal measure.

The leaders who succeed in such environments are those who replace positional authority with relational capital. They know that escalation is not a signal of weakness, but a declaration of alignment, a commitment to the collective outcome over individual comfort. They escalate not to assign blame, but to synchronize decisions across invisible boundaries.

And yet, the complexity of matrixed organizations also makes them vulnerable during crises. When urgency replaces deliberation and risk amplifies across functions, escalation moves from strategic to existential. The next chapter explores these high-stakes moments — when timing is tight, stakes are high, and escalation becomes not just a choice, but a responsibility.

Matrix organizations are like webs, pull one thread, and vibrations are felt across continents. Escalating in such environments requires **extra precision**: inform both solid and dotted lines, respect cultural tones, use asynchronous tools, and above all, build the political capital that ensures your voice carries weight.

"Matrix escalation is a chess game—patience and strategy win." – Anonymous

---

CHAPTER 7
ESCALATION IN CRISES / HIGH-STAKES SITUATIONS

"In the midst of chaos, there is also opportunity." – Sun Tzu

Crises compress time, magnify stakes, and strip away the comfort of process. In such moments, escalation becomes not just a tool but a lifeline. A missed delivery in routine projects may inconvenience; in a high-stakes crisis, it can topple client relationships, trigger financial penalties, or even end careers.

This chapter explores how escalation transforms under pressure: faster, sharper, and more visible.

"A crisis is the true test of leadership — it strips away rhetoric and reveals resolve." — Warren Bennis

---

1. The Nature of Crisis Escalation

- **High visibility**: Executives, boards, sometimes even regulators are watching.
- **No buffer time**: Decisions must be made in hours, not weeks.
- **Reputational risk**: Beyond the issue itself, *how* escalation is handled can shape stakeholder trust for years.

In crises, leaders are often more forgiving of bad news than of late news. The cardinal sin is to sit on a problem until it explodes.

---

2. Principles of Crisis Escalation

- **Speed over perfection**: Share what you know, caveat what you don't.
- **Escalate up and across**: Loop in parallel stakeholders — legal, compliance, PR, not just your line manager.
- **Clarity of message**: Replace "we are working on it" with "current status: X; immediate risk: Y; next step: Z."
- **Tone of accountability**: Take ownership of what is within your control, even if the cause lies elsewhere.

---

3. Scenarios and Mini Caselets

a) Cybersecurity Breach

A financial services firm discovers a system breach at 2:00 a.m. The IT head must decide: escalate immediately to the CEO and regulator, or wait until the investigation confirms the scale?

- *Best practice:* Escalate immediately, framing it as "potential breach under investigation" with hourly updates. Transparency protects trust.

---

b) Client Outage in a Technology Firm

A data center outage brings down a Fortune 100 client's systems.

- Poor escalation: *"We're still looking into it; no update yet."*
- Effective escalation: *"Outage identified at 02:43 GMT, affecting client A. Root cause under investigation. Current ETA for restoration: 4 hours. Dedicated team on-site. Next update in 30 minutes."*

---

c) Public Relations Crisis

A product defect triggers viral backlash on social media. Marketing wants to "wait it out," but the risk team pushes for escalation.

- Lesson: Silence in public crises is escalation delayed, and in reputational crises, delay equals damage.

---

4. The Crisis Escalation Ladder

A practical framework for action under stress:

1. **Identify**: Detect anomaly or risk.
2. **Inform**: Escalate to immediate leadership + parallel functions.
3. **Involve**: Pull in expertise — legal, PR, regulators if needed.
4. **Instruct**: Share next steps, update cadence, and escalation tree.

5. **Iterate**: Keep communication flowing until resolution.

Closing Thought

"In a crisis, don't hide. Communicate."
— Rudy Giuliani

In moments of crisis, escalation stops being a leadership option and becomes a leadership duty. The speed of decisions, the precision of words, and the steadiness of tone define not only outcomes but reputations. Crises strip away process and expose instinct, showing who can stay composed when clarity is most clouded.

The case studies in this chapter reveal a simple truth: escalation in a crisis is not about reacting faster; it is about *responding wiser*. The best leaders don't merely transmit urgency, they translate it. They bring focus to confusion, order to noise, and accountability to chaos. Their calm presence becomes the signal others tune into when systems and structures begin to fail.

Yet even the most seasoned leaders stumble when escalation is improvised. Pressure amplifies emotion, and words said in haste can escalate the wrong way. That is why every organization needs a vocabulary for crisis, a way to communicate facts without fuelling fear.

Crises are accelerators of both failure and credibility. Those who escalate swiftly, responsibly, and transparently are remembered not as messengers of doom but as leaders who protected the organization in its darkest hours.

As we move to the next chapter, we turn these lessons into practice — exploring *templates and scripts* that help professionals articulate escalation with precision, empathy, and authority. Because in the storm of a crisis, clarity of communication is not just a skill — it is survival.

> ***"Escalation in crisis is about light, not heat." – Anonymous***

CHAPTER 8

ESCALATION TEMPLATES AND SCRIPTS

"Words are, in my not-so-humble opinion, our most inexhaustible source of magic." – J.K. Rowling

Scripts and templates provide consistency in escalation. An email escalation should focus on facts, context, and the ask, avoiding blame while directing attention toward resolution.

Escalation is as much an **art of communication** as it is a process of problem-solving. A poorly crafted escalation — blunt, emotional, or without context can backfire, creating defensiveness instead of resolution. Conversely, a well-structured escalation, framed with precision and professionalism, can open doors, accelerate decision-making, and preserve relationships.

"The single biggest problem in communication is the illusion that it has taken place." — George Bernard Shaw

In this chapter, I will share a few **ready-to-use templates** and **scripts** that professionals can adapt depending on the context: from project bottlenecks to crises. These are not "fill-in-the-blank" tools; they are **communication frameworks** that allow you to tailor tone, content, and urgency to your specific situation.

---

1. Anatomy of a Strong Escalation Communication and Decision matrix

Every effective escalation — whether verbal, email, or formal memo — has four essential ingredients:

Context — "Here's what's happening."

A clean, factual backdrop. No emotion. No exaggeration. Just a simple narrative that positions the issue.

Impact — "Here's why it matters."

Escalation gains meaning when linked to consequences — timelines, stakeholder deliverables, compliance, risk.

Ask — "Here's what I need."

A clear request signals maturity.
It shows that escalation is not a complaint but a leadership act aimed at resolution.

Evidence — "Here's what supports this."

Evidence is the grounding rod of credibility.
It prevents defensiveness and keeps the conversation objective.

Think of this as the **C-I-A-E framework**: *Context · Impact · Ask · Evidence.*

---

2. Email Escalation Templates

A. Project Bottleneck — "Polite but Firm" Escalation

Subject: Escalation: Pending Dependencies Affecting [Project Name] Timeline

Dear [Manager/Senior Leader],

I'd like to bring to your attention a critical dependency affecting the progress of [Project Name]. Despite repeated follow-ups with [Team/Owner], the deliverable [specific item] remains pending.

Context: This deliverable was due on [date] and is required for [specific milestone].
Impact: The delay has now placed the project timeline at risk, potentially impacting [costs/client commitment/launch date].
Ask: I request your intervention to expedite the resolution of this dependency. A timely decision or resource allocation will help us recover lost ground.

I've attached a tracker for reference, highlighting pending items and owners. Happy to provide more details as needed.

Best regards,
[Your Name]

Why this works: It is respectful, fact-driven, and outcome-oriented. It avoids blame and gives the recipient a clear action point.

B. People Issue — "Tone-sensitive" Escalation

Subject: Escalation: Support Required on Team Collaboration Concern

Dear [HR/Manager],

I'd like to formally escalate a concern regarding collaboration within [Team/Project]. Despite direct discussions with

[Individual's Name] to resolve the issue, challenges persist, affecting delivery quality and team morale.

Context: The issue primarily concerns [specific behaviour/conflict].
Impact: This is delaying deliverables, creating stress across the team, and impacting client confidence.
Ask: I request your guidance and intervention to help mediate this situation before it further escalates.

I remain committed to constructive resolution and have documented key incidents for transparency.

Regards,
[Your Name]

Why this works: It acknowledges prior attempts at self-resolution, avoids personal attacks, and frames the escalation as a professional request for support.

C. Crisis Escalation — "Urgent, No-Nonsense" Template

Subject: URGENT Escalation: Immediate Risk to [Business/Client/Operations]

Dear [Executive/Senior Stakeholder],

This is to immediately escalate a critical risk: [describe incident in 2–3 sentences].

Facts: [Describe what has happened, verified details only.]
Impact: This poses a direct risk to [safety, compliance, client operations, or financial exposure].

Ask: We require an urgent decision on [specific action] within the next [time window].

I have activated the immediate response team and attached a brief incident summary. Please advise on next steps.

Regards,
[Your Name]

Why this works: In high-stakes moments, brevity, and clarity matter more than politeness. This format creates urgency without panic.

---

3. Verbal Escalation Scripts (Boardroom & Meetings)

Sometimes escalation happens not in writing but in the heat of a meeting. Here are scripts that demonstrate confidence without aggression.

- **In a Steering Committee Meeting**
  "Before we proceed, I'd like to escalate a concern. The budget allocation for [initiative] is now creating downstream risks. Unless we address this in the next two weeks, we risk derailing [major milestone/client delivery]. May I request the committee's direction on whether we can reallocate resources or adjust the scope?"

- **In a One-on-One with a Senior Leader**
  "I've attempted to resolve this with [X team], but the issue persists. It's now impacting deliverables. I'd like your support in either intervening directly or helping unlock the right resources to move forward."

- **In a Cross-functional Meeting**
  "I don't want to delay the discussion, but for transparency, I need to escalate this dependency. If we don't resolve ownership of [task] today, the delivery timeline will slip. Can we agree on next steps now?"

---

4. Escalation Scripts for Different Media

- **Instant Messaging (Slack/Teams):**
  "Hi [Name], quick escalation: [issue] is blocking [task]. Can you help prioritize this today, or should I escalate to [senior leader] for support?"

- **Formal Memo:**
  Used for compliance/regulatory escalations. It is longer, structured, and follows official templates (with incident details, evidence, timelines, and impact analysis).

---

5. Escalation Closing Scripts

Every escalation should end with **resolution language** that closes the loop and keeps relationships intact.

Examples:

- *"Thank you for your intervention. With your support, the issue is now resolved."*

- *"I appreciate your time on this matter; the quick action has helped us stay on track."*

- *"While the situation was challenging, the escalation ensured transparency and swift resolution."*

Every effective escalation should end with resolution language — words that close the loop, protect trust, and keep relationships intact. And as we will see throughout this book, relationships are often the real currency of escalation; they determine not just the outcome, but how that outcome is experienced. That is why, although CIAE is introduced here as a practical structure — Context, Impact, Ask, Evidence — the framework does not remain static. As escalations become more complex, the final 'E' expands to include empathy, creating CIAE+, where evidence grounds the message and empathy ensures it can be received without damaging the relationship.

Evidence is essential in early escalations.
It ensures credibility.
It strips away misunderstanding.
It anchors the message in facts, not feelings.

But as communication becomes more nuanced — especially across teams, cultures, senior stakeholders, and high-stakes conversations — the final "E" gradually expands.

It grows from **Evidence** into **Evidence + Empathy**.

***"The art of communication is the language of leadership."* — James Humes**

Closing Thought

In this chapter, we translated the art of escalation into the language of action — turning reflection into response. From the first line of an escalation email to the tone of a difficult call, we learned that communication is not just about words, but about intent expressed with precision.

Templates and scripts are not mechanical tools; they are frameworks for empathy. They ensure that emotion doesn't overpower evidence and that urgency doesn't eclipse respect. A well-crafted escalation note or dialogue isn't about control, it's about clarity. It signals professionalism, invites collaboration, and prevents conflict from hardening into confrontation.

Yet, no script can replace judgment. The best communicators personalize structure with sincerity. They know when to use brevity, when to explain context, and when silence can speak louder than any sentence. The true art lies in balancing tact with transparency.

Escalations are not just about raising problems; they are about **leading conversations toward resolution**. With the right templates and scripts, escalation becomes not an act of confrontation, but a **catalyst for progress**.

Escalation succeeds or collapses on communication. CIAE helps you shape the message:

> Begin with **Context**, show the **Impact**, articulate the **Ask**, and support it with **Evidence**.

But as you advance through this book, you'll discover that the most powerful escalations, especially those involving people, pressure, and politics — require something more.

They require empathy. Not instead of evidence, but alongside it.

This is where CIAE quietly evolves into **CIAE+** — a communication lens that balances truth with tact, and clarity with compassion.

Understanding CIAE makes you effective. Embracing CIAE+ makes you influential.

As we move ahead, we shift focus from *what* to say to *whom* to say it to, and more importantly, *how*. In the next chapter, we explore the nuances of **escalating upward** a leadership tightrope where clarity must coexist with respect, and where managing perception becomes as critical as managing the message.

"Scripts keep emotions from writing the story." – Corporate Saying

Chapter 9
Escalating Up Without Backlash

"You can tell a lot about a person by how they handle a rainy day, lost luggage, and tangled Christmas lights." – Maya Angelou

Escalating upward requires diplomacy. It must show respect while making the seriousness clear. The art lies in protecting relationships while surfacing truth.

Escalating upward is the **most delicate form of escalation**. When you raise concerns to senior leadership, particularly about their own decisions, priorities, or even behaviour, the stakes are higher. Careers can be made or unmade not by what you escalate, but by **how** you escalate.

"Power's real test is not how loudly you speak, but how well you can be heard when you speak softly." — Anonymous Corporate Saying

This chapter focuses on the fine art of "managing up" while protecting your professional credibility and relationships.

---

1. Managing Upward — Respectfully

Escalating upward doesn't mean bypassing levels or challenging authority head-on. It is about **framing issues in a way that leaders see alignment, not opposition.**

Subtle strategies to manage upward escalation:

- **Anchor to Business Outcomes:** Frame the escalation in terms of the company's goals — cost, revenue, client satisfaction, compliance. Example: *"To deliver on Q3 commitments, we may need your help prioritizing X over Y."*
- **Ask, Don't Accuse:** Turn escalations into requests for guidance. Instead of *"This won't work"*, try: *"How do you suggest we proceed, given [constraint]?"*
- **Package the Pain with Options:** Leaders appreciate problems, but they value solutions more. Present at least **two alternative paths**, with pros and cons, instead of dumping the issue at their desk.
- **Respect Chain of Command (when possible):** Even when escalating upward, inform your immediate manager. Surprises create friction; alignment builds trust.

Example Dialogue:
"We've tried X and Y with limited success. I'd like your guidance on whether you see merit in pursuing Z, given the impact on timeline. This ensures we stay aligned with leadership intent."

---

2. CYA (Cover Your Actions) Without Blame-Shifting

Every escalation carries the unspoken subtext: *"Who dropped the ball?"*

If you're not careful, escalation can look like blame-shifting. The art is to **protect yourself (CYA) without damaging others unnecessarily**.

Best practices:

- **Document Decisions, Not Accusations:** Instead of *"Finance failed to share numbers"*, write: *"Data from Finance, due on [date], is still pending; this delays our ability to finalize forecasts."*
- **Be Transparent About Your Actions:** Clearly state what you did to address the issue before escalating: *"I reached out to [X] twice, last on [date], but haven't received an update."*
- **Escalate Systems, Not Individuals:** Focus on broken processes, not people. Leaders prefer fixing leaks in the pipeline, not conducting witch hunts.
- **Balance Accountability:** If someone is at fault, state facts neutrally, avoiding emotional tone. Let leadership connect the dots.

Example Language:

"We attempted resolution at the working level by clarifying dependencies with Team X and revising timelines. Despite these efforts, the risk remains. Escalating now to avoid downstream impact on [project/client]."

This keeps the focus on the **issue**, not personalities.

3. Escalating on Leadership Behaviour — The Last Resort

The most sensitive escalation is when the **behaviour of leadership itself** is the issue — harassment, toxic conduct, ethical lapses, or decisions that risk compliance.

This is not routine escalation; it is a **last resort.**

Guidelines for escalating leadership behaviour:

- **Know the Threshold:** This is not about minor disagreements or stylistic differences; escalate only for significant ethical, legal, or cultural breaches.
- **Leverage Formal Channels:** HR, Ethics Committees, Ombudsman programs — these exist for a reason.
- **Document Meticulously:** Dates, times, witnesses, and impact. Avoid hearsay.
- **Protect Yourself:** If escalation involves power misuse, escalate through confidential or whistleblower mechanisms.
- **Expect Fallout, Prepare Resilience:** Even in mature organizations, this path can be career-shaping. Ensure you have mentors, allies, and clarity of intent.

Example Script (to HR/Ethics Office):

"I am raising this formally as it concerns behaviour inconsistent with our code of conduct. While I respect the leadership hierarchy, I believe this matter requires independent review for the safety and integrity of the workplace."

This type of escalation is about **principles over politics**. Done right, it may not only protect you but also preserve the organization's credibility.

Closing Thought

Escalating upward is one of the most courageous acts in corporate life, and one of the most misunderstood. It demands a rare combination of conviction, composure, and context. Unlike horizontal or procedural escalations, upward escalation is personal; it tests the boundaries of hierarchy and the maturity of culture.

Through this chapter, we examined that delicate balance — the art of voicing a concern without appearing confrontational, and of standing firm without being seen as insubordinate. We explored how preparation, documentation, and framing can turn escalation from a challenge to authority into a commitment to accountability. When managed well, it strengthens trust; when mishandled, it fractures it.

Escalation upward is not about proving someone wrong, it is about ensuring that decisions align with principles and that silence never becomes complicity. It requires self-awareness to separate ego from ethics and diplomacy to ensure that message and motive stay aligned. True professionals escalate up not to protect themselves, but to protect the integrity of the organization.

Yet, even with all preparation, escalation across senior lines carries risk — of perception, power, and politics. How this act is received often depends not only on hierarchy but also on *culture*. In some contexts, directness is valued; in others, it is interpreted as disrespect.

Escalating upward is less about courage and more about **craftsmanship**. Done poorly, it can look like insubordination. Done well, it demonstrates maturity, integrity, and alignment with organizational goals.

In the next chapter, we explore these nuances — how cultural values, communication norms, and leadership archetypes shape the way escalation is understood across the world.

> ***“"You don’t raise your voice; you improve your argument."***
> ***— Desmond Tutu***

CHAPTER 10

ESCALATION ACROSS CULTURES (GLOBAL CONTEXTS)

"Culture eats strategy for breakfast."
– Peter Drucker

Escalation looks different across cultures. In some Asian contexts, direct escalation is seen as disrespectful, while in Western settings, silence can be perceived as incompetence. Leaders must adapt their escalation strategies to cultural norms.

In a globalized workplace, escalation is rarely a one-size-fits-all exercise. What might be seen as proactive in one culture can be viewed as disrespectful in another. Escalation across cultures is about **reading context, respecting norms, and flexing your style without compromising the message**.

"Culture is the lens through which we see problems, and the filter through which we decide how loudly to raise them." — Adapted from Geert Hofstede

---

1. Cultural Dimensions of Escalation

Drawing from Hofstede's and Erin Meyer's frameworks on cultural differences, escalation behaviours can be shaped by:

- **Power Distance:**
    - In **high power-distance cultures** (e.g., India, China, UAE), escalation upward is often formal, hierarchical, and heavily documented. Jumping levels is seen as disrespectful unless protocol is followed.
    - In **low power-distance cultures** (e.g., US, Netherlands, Australia), upward escalation is expected to be direct and pragmatic — "open door" policies are real.
- **Communication Style:**
    - **Direct cultures** (e.g., Germany, US, Israel) value explicit facts, even if blunt.
    - **Indirect cultures** (e.g., Japan, India, parts of Latin America) prefer nuance, suggestion, and diplomacy. An escalation may come as a "hint" rather than a hard statement.
- **Conflict Tolerance:**
    - In some cultures, conflict is viewed as healthy debate (e.g., France, US).
    - In others, conflict is to be avoided, so escalation is framed as consensus-seeking (e.g., Japan, Thailand).
- **Time Orientation:**
    - Escalation urgency differs. A "24-hour escalation" in the US might translate to

"within a week" in more flexible, relationship-driven cultures.

---

2. Escalation Nuances Across Regions

United States / Western Europe

- Escalation is expected as part of accountability.
- Direct, concise, and fact-driven messages are valued.
- Leaders see escalation as problem-solving, not insubordination.

Example boardroom phrase:
"I need to escalate this risk so we can make a timely decision before it affects delivery."

Japan

- Escalation is subtle and often happens "off the record."
- Indirect language is used to save face.
- Formal escalation may go through multiple layers of consensus (Nema Washi) *.

* *Nema Washi* is a Japanese term for an informal, consensus-building process of laying the groundwork for a major project or decision. It involves communicating with key stakeholders and decision-makers beforehand to build support, gather feedback, and ensure a smooth process once a formal proposal is made.

Example phrase:
"Perhaps we should explore another perspective before moving ahead, as there may be some concerns down the line."

India

- Formal escalation is accepted but should follow hierarchy.
- Tone matters: respectful, deferential, with context.
- Often backed with heavy documentation to avoid appearing personal.

Example phrase:
"In the interest of meeting client commitments, I'd like to seek your guidance on how we can unblock this dependency."

Middle East / Africa

- Respect for authority is critical. Escalations must show loyalty to leadership.
- Relationships often precede escalation: private discussions are preferred before formal channels.

Example phrase:
"Out of respect for timelines and the team's effort, I feel it's important to bring this to your attention now."

France / Southern Europe

- Debate and challenge are culturally accepted.

- Escalations can be passionate, but intellectual framing is valued.

Example phrase:
"We must escalate this issue, otherwise the integrity of the project will be compromised."

---

3. Strategies for Cross-Cultural Escalations

- **Do your cultural homework:** Before escalating in a global team, understand local norms.
- **Mirror the recipient's style:** Match tone and format to the leader's preferred communication style (concise vs detailed, formal vs informal).
- **Leverage local allies:** Sometimes it's better to channel your escalation through someone culturally closer to the recipient.
- **Use universal anchors:** Business impact, compliance, client satisfaction — these transcend cultures.

---

4. Risks and Rewards of Cross-Cultural Escalation

- **Risks:** Being perceived as too aggressive, bypassing hierarchy, or creating reputational damage.
- **Rewards:** Demonstrating global maturity, building credibility across regions, and showing cultural intelligence — often a leadership differentiator.

Closing Thought

"The essence of cross-cultural leadership is not to erase differences, but to navigate them with respect and clarity." — Erin Meyer

In this chapter, we travelled beyond geography to understand how culture silently codes communication. From the direct candour of Western workplaces to the nuanced restraint of Asian workplaces, we discovered that escalation is never a universal act, it is a cultural interpretation of courage. What feels like transparency in one culture may seem like confrontation in another; what appears as respect in one context may be perceived as avoidance in another.

The case discussions reminded us that global leaders operate not only across time zones but across emotional landscapes. They must learn to read pauses as carefully as they read emails, to sense hesitation behind politeness, and to differentiate disagreement from dissent. Escalation, in its truest form, is not about imposing one's communication style — it is about decoding another's.

Culturally intelligent escalation begins with curiosity. It requires listening without judgment and framing without assumption. The most effective leaders are those who adapt their approach — adjusting tone, timing, and channel, without compromising on authenticity or ethics. They build trust by understanding that communication is not just what is said, but how it is heard.

Escalating across cultures is not about changing the message, it is about **changing the packaging**. When you adapt tone, format, and approach, your escalation travels farther, lands better, and achieves results without backlash.

As we step into the next chapter, we explore how this cultural complexity now merges with technology. The rise of remote work, digital collaboration tools, and AI-driven communication has created a new layer of challenge — one where tone can be lost in text, emotion can be misread by machines, and escalation must evolve for a world that never sleeps.

"Global escalation succeeds when empathy precedes urgency."
– Corporate Wisdom

CHAPTER 11

DIGITAL ESCALATIONS (ESCALATING IN THE AGE OF REMOTE WORK & AI)

"Technology is a useful servant but a dangerous master." – Christian Lous Lange

Remote work and AI-driven workflows have changed escalation. Now, tone in emails or chat tools carries outsized weight. Digital escalations must be concise, transparent, and culturally neutral.

In the modern workplace, escalation is no longer confined to boardrooms or hushed corridor conversations. With distributed teams, remote-first cultures, and digital communication tools, escalation now happens through **screens, chat windows, emails, and AI-powered platforms**.

While digital tools make escalation faster, they also amplify risks: tone can be misread, urgency mistaken for hostility, and once an escalation is "on record," it lives forever in archives and screenshots. This chapter explores how to escalate effectively — and safely — in a digital-first world.

"Technology doesn't change human nature; it magnifies it." — Clay Shirky

---

1. The New Landscape of Digital Escalation

- **Remote Teams:** With global, virtual teams, leaders are rarely in the same room. Escalations are asynchronous, often email or chat based.
- **Always-On Communication:** Slack, Teams, WhatsApp blur work-life boundaries — escalation messages may arrive at 11 pm. Timing is as critical as tone.
- **AI as a Mediator:** From predictive analytics flagging risks to AI-driven workflow escalations, "machines" now sometimes escalate issues before humans do.
- **Documentation by Default:** Unlike verbal escalations, digital escalations create **permanent records** — a blessing for accountability, a curse for reputation.

---

2. Principles of Effective Digital Escalation

- **Clarity Over Brevity:** Avoid cryptic one-liners in Slack or email. What feels efficient may seem curt or aggressive.
- **Tone-Checking:** Read your escalation twice before hitting send. Emojis may soften tone in peer chats, but in formal escalation emails, they diminish credibility.

- **Channel Discipline:** Escalate in the **right channel**:
    - Quick blockers → Slack/Teams DM
    - Formal dependencies → Email with documentation
    - High-risk issues → Escalation tools/ticketing systems
- **Asynchronous Sensitivity:** Consider time zones. Sending a midnight escalation email may feel urgent but creates stress for colleagues waking up to a crisis.

---

3. Escalation in Remote-First Meetings

In Zoom, Teams, or WebEx, escalation has its own challenges:

- **Body Language Is Lost:** Without physical cues, escalation may sound sharper than intended. Use measured tone and deliberate pauses.
- **Escalate in Agenda, Not Ambush:** If possible, flag the escalation in advance — *"I'll need 5 minutes to raise a project risk."*
- **Record for Transparency:** In sensitive escalations, ensure the meeting is recorded or minutes are circulated. This protects against selective memory.

Example Script in Remote Meeting:
"I'd like to escalate a concern for visibility. Despite repeated attempts at resolution, the dependency from Team X remains unresolved, and it

threatens our milestone delivery. I'd appreciate leadership guidance on next steps."

---

4. AI and Automated Escalations

AI is reshaping how escalations surface:

- **Predictive Risk Escalations:** Project management tools (e.g., Jira, MS Project, Asana) now auto-flag delays, escalating them before humans' notice.
- **Compliance Alerts:** AI-driven monitoring tools escalate suspicious financial or security activity to leadership instantly.
- **Bias Risks:** Algorithms may mis-prioritize escalations, flagging false positives or overlooking nuanced human issues.

Guideline: Always **humanize the machine's escalation**. Add context, judgment, and framing before forwarding AI-generated alerts up the chain.

---

5. Digital Escalation Pitfalls to Avoid

- **Escalating in Public Channels:** Posting escalation in group Slack channels can shame teams — use DMs or structured emails instead.
- **Overusing "URGENT" Tags:** If everything is marked urgent, nothing is. Leaders start ignoring your messages.

- **Escalating Emotionally:** Digital text strips nuance; frustration comes across as hostility.
- **The "Reply-All Bomb":** Escalating by CC'ing half the company is less about resolution and more about politics — and rarely works in your favour.

---

6. Best Practices Checklist

Before hitting *Send* on a digital escalation, ask:

1. Is this the right channel?
2. Am I clear on context, facts, impact, and ask?
3. Could this be misread as hostile or defensive?
4. Have I documented prior attempts at resolution?
5. Am I okay with this email/chat being read aloud in a boardroom a year from now?

If yes, escalate. If not, revise.

Closing Thought

"The digital record is unforgiving — make sure your escalation is something you'd defend even if projected on the big screen." **— Modern Corporate Maxim**

The digital age has redefined escalation. What was once a face-to-face dialogue now unfolds in pixels — through messages, pings, and emails that travel faster than thought and linger longer than intent. In this hyperconnected world, escalation is no longer about reaching the right person; it's about ensuring the message survives the medium.

As we explored in this chapter, the shift to remote work and digital collaboration has created a paradox. Technology promises transparency but often delivers misinterpretation. Tone is flattened, empathy is filtered out, and the human cues that soften escalation — a pause, a sigh, a glance, are replaced by text that can be read ten different ways. The risk is not only miscommunication, but *misperception.*

Yet, technology is not the enemy of empathy — it is its amplifier, if used wisely. The leaders who thrive in digital ecosystems are those who write as they speak: with clarity, restraint, and humanity. They know that escalation online must carry the same discipline as escalation in person — anchored in facts, framed with respect, and followed through with dialogue.

The rise of AI adds another dimension. Machines may soon flag anomalies faster than humans can, but no algorithm can yet gauge the emotion behind a decision to escalate or stay silent. The future will therefore belong to professionals who combine *digital fluency* with *emotional literacy.* Don't forget tone, polite escalation is still escalation.

In the digital age, escalation is no longer a fleeting conversation. It is a **permanent footprint of your professionalism, judgment, and credibility**. Mastering this new landscape means learning not just when to escalate, but **how to package escalation for a world where every word is searchable, storable, and shareable**.

Playbook Box: Do's & Don'ts of Digital Escalations

Do's

- Use private channels for first escalations.
- Structure emails for clarity: Subject → Risk → Impact → Action Needed.
- Tag urgency appropriately (#Critical, #Blocker).
- Use delayed send to avoid time zone clashes.
- Keep a clean digital trail.

Don'ts

- Don't escalate in public chat unless it's a systemic blocker.
- Don't rely on emojis or CAPS to signal urgency.
- Don't overuse escalation tags — they lose meaning.
- Don't assume AI triage means a human has seen your issue.

As we move to the next chapter, we explore the other side of escalation — **de-escalation**. For in a world of constant communication, knowing when and how to *cool the temperature* is often a greater act of leadership than knowing when to turn up the heat.

> ***"Digital escalation is clarity typed, not chaos clicked." – Anonymous***

Chapter 12

De-escalation as a Skill

"Speak when you are angry and you will make the best speech you will ever regret." – Ambrose Bierce

De-escalation is as critical as escalation. Cooling down conflict, mediating between peers, and redirecting conversations toward solutions are leadership superpowers.

Escalation is a powerful tool, but unchecked, it can spiral into confrontation. That's where **de-escalation** becomes not just a complementary skill, but an essential one. If escalation is the art of raising an issue, de-escalation is the craft of cooling it down without losing momentum.

Corporate environments thrive on pressure — deadlines, budgets, performance metrics. With so many moving parts, friction is inevitable. But escalation doesn't always mean escalating *up*. Sometimes, the wiser course is to de-escalate sideways, diffusing heat before it burns bridges.

"Anyone can make a crisis worse; leaders are remembered for those moments when they made it better." – Anonymous

---

Why De-escalation Matters

1. **Preserving Relationships**
   - Today's adversary in a heated escalation could be tomorrow's ally in a critical project.
   - De-escalation helps ensure you win the war without alienating allies.
2. **Avoiding Escalation Fatigue**
   - Leaders faced with constant escalations may tune out.
   - Strategic de-escalation ensures attention is focused only on genuine critical issues.
3. **Reputation Management**
   - Escalators who never de-escalate are seen as alarmists.
   - The ability to calm tensions showcases maturity and leadership readiness.

The Three Faces of De-escalation

1. **Cooling Down After the Heat**
   - A tense email exchange doesn't always need a bigger CC list.
   - Often, what's needed is a phone call with the line: *"Let's align offline before this snowballs."*

- Corporate nuance: Pausing escalation isn't weakness — it signals confidence that you can resolve things directly.

2. **Mediating Between Peers**
    - In matrix organizations, peers can be locked in a stalemate.
    - Example dialogue:
        - *Peer A*: "Your team missed the deadline — this is unacceptable."
        - *Peer B*: "We flagged the dependency weeks ago; you ignored it."
        - *Mediator*: "I hear both sides. Let's focus on what's needed to move forward: [X deliverable by Y date]."
    - De-escalation here is about **shifting the conversation from blame to solution.**
3. **Redirecting Toward Resolution**
    - When escalation is inevitable, de-escalation reframes tone.
    - Instead of: *"We're blocked, and this will fail unless leadership intervenes,"*
      Try: *"We're facing a challenge that risks timelines. Here are two proposed solutions. Leadership input will help us align on the best path."*
    - This transforms escalation from a complaint into a call for collaboration.

Practical Tactics for De-escalation

- **Use the pause.** Delay your reply by 30 minutes — urgency rarely justifies an emotional response.
- **Mirror back facts.** Summarize what both sides have said without judgment; this lowers tension.
- **Offer face time.** Even in digital-first workplaces, a quick video call can humanize both parties.
- **Acknowledge emotions but focus on impact.**
    - *"I can see this has been frustrating. Let's focus on what's blocking us now."*
- **Create small wins.** Break a conflict into a solvable first step — nothing de-escalates like progress.

Real-World Example

A global sales leader once escalated a missed product delivery in a furious all-hands email. Instead of firing back defensively, the product manager called him directly. Within 15 minutes, the Project Manager reframed the issue:

- Delivery was delayed due to a compliance recheck.
- Short-term workaround was proposed.
- Joint communication was drafted for the client.

By **de-escalating** first, the Project Manager turned a potential reputation crisis into a shared problem-solving win.

Closing Thought

The true measure of a leader is not how loudly they escalate, but how calmly they de-escalate. In the heat of conflict, when words have hardened and tempers rise, the ability to cool the temperature without extinguishing engagement defines emotional maturity. De-escalation, as we explored in this chapter, is not about surrender — it is about stewardship. It is the act of restoring focus when distraction takes over.

We have seen how de-escalation requires presence — the discipline to listen fully, to separate emotion from evidence, and to redirect conversations toward solutions rather than blame. It calls for courage, patience, and empathy — the kind that understands that people don't argue against facts; they react to how facts make them feel.

De-escalation transforms conflict into collaboration by shifting the narrative from who is right to what is right. It builds trust not through authority, but through authenticity. When practiced consistently, it turns potential escalations into teachable moments, and strained relationships into resilient ones.

Yet, de-escalation is not instinctive — it is learned. It demands the same rigor as escalation itself, but with a different energy: less heat, more light.

Playbook Box: De-escalation Do's & Don'ts

Do's

- Do pick up the phone before replying to an escalation email.
- Do summarize facts neutrally to reduce heat.

- Do propose solutions, not just apologies.
- Do recognize emotions without inflaming them.
- Do redirect the group's energy toward the common goal.

Don'ts

- Don't copy more people just to "win the thread."
- Don't dismiss the issue as "not important" — it will backfire.
- Don't escalate tone in writing (sarcasm, CAPS, bolding).
- Don't delay too long, silence fuels escalation.
- Don't confuse de-escalation with surrender.

"The measure of leadership is not how loudly you escalate, but how skilfully you can turn noise into progress."

In the next chapter, we translate this emotional intelligence into leadership frameworks. The **Escalation Playbook for Leaders** brings together everything we've explored — tools, rules, tone, and temperament — and shows how great leaders institutionalize escalation and de-escalation as twin pillars of trust and performance.

"De-escalation is leadership in slow motion." – Anonymous

CHAPTER 13
THE ESCALATION PLAYBOOK FOR LEADERS

"Leadership is not about being in charge. It is about taking care of those in your charge." – Simon Sinek

Leaders must institutionalize escalation frameworks: clear policies, open-door cultures, and mechanisms to encourage early surfacing of issues.

"The true test of leadership is not in avoiding escalation but in how you respond when it arrives at your desk." – Anonymous

Escalation is not just an employee's tool, it is a mirror for leadership. Every escalation tells a story: about the organization's culture, its processes, and its ability to handle pressure. For leaders, escalations are both a responsibility and an opportunity. Handled well, they build trust and resilience. Handled poorly, they create fear, silence, or chaos.

The Leader's Dilemma

Leaders often find themselves walking a tightrope:

- **Encourage escalations too openly,** and you risk being overwhelmed with noise.

- **Discourage escalations too strongly,** and you breed silence — problems fester until they explode.

The real art is in striking the balance — ensuring escalations are welcomed, but only when they add value.

How Leaders Should Receive Escalations

1. **Pause Before Reacting**
    - A leader's first reaction sets the tone. Dismissing an escalation immediately signals "don't bother me again."
    - Instead: *"Thank you for raising this — let's look at the facts together."*
2. **Acknowledge Without Blame**
    - Escalations often come loaded with frustration. Leaders must separate the signal (facts) from the noise (emotion).
    - *"I understand this has been challenging. Let's focus on the root cause."*
3. **Validate the Escalation Path**
    - Check: Did the individual try resolving before escalating?
    - If yes → reward transparency.
    - If no → coach on the right sequence.

Filtering Genuine Issues from Noise

Not every escalation is equal. Leaders need triage skills.

- **Type 1: Legitimate Risk**
  - Example: Regulatory non-compliance flagged.
  - Action: Immediate intervention.
- **Type 2: Process Gap**
  - Example: Teams unclear on accountability.
  - Action: Clarify roles, refine process.
- **Type 3: Personality Clash**
  - Example: Peer conflict escalated without attempts at mediation.
  - Action: Send back for peer resolution.
- **Type 4: Escalation-as-Leverage**
  - Example: Employee escalates prematurely to gain advantage.
  - Action: Coach on escalation ethics.

How Leaders Should Respond

1. **Be Firm, Not Defensive**
   - *Bad response: "Why wasn't I told earlier?"*
   - *Better response: "Okay, now that it's surfaced, here's how we'll fix it."*

2. **Make It Constructive**
    - Use escalation as a trigger to fix root causes, not just the immediate fire.
3. **Communicate Resolution Widely**
    - Share how the escalation was handled — this builds trust in the process.

Boardroom Dialogue Example

- **Manager:** *"We've escalated because the compliance deadline is at risk, and we don't have sign-off."*
- **Leader (wrong response):** *"Why do I always hear about these issues last minute?"*
- **Leader (right response):** *"Thank you for flagging this early enough. Let's define what support is needed now, and then we'll review how to prevent this next cycle."*

The contrast highlights how leaders can either shut down or strengthen the escalation culture.

The Leader's Playbook: Building a Healthy Escalation Culture

- Set **clear escalation channels** (who, when, how).
- Reward **early and appropriate escalations** — they save time, money, and reputation.
- Train managers to act as **first-line de-escalators** before things reach the top.

- Avoid "shooting the messenger" — people will simply stop bringing you bad news.
- Demonstrate transparency: When you escalate upwards (e.g., to the board), role-model how it should be done.

Playbook Box: Do's & Don'ts for Leaders Handling Escalations

Do's

- Do listen fully before judging.
- Do separate facts from emotion.
- Do appreciate timely escalations.
- Do act decisively and communicate outcomes.
- Do use escalations to fix root causes, not just patch symptoms.

Don'ts

- Don't punish the messenger.
- Don't dismiss without review.
- Don't allow escalation to become a shortcut for every issue.
- Don't hoard escalations, escalate further if needed.
- Don't forget: silence in your organisation may signal fear, not harmony.

Closing Thought

Leadership is not defined by the absence of conflict, but by the ability to manage it with integrity and composure. The most successful leaders do not avoid escalations, they design systems that make them purposeful, timely, and fair. This chapter brought together the tools, principles, and mindsets that help transform escalation from a reaction into a rhythm — one that protects performance while preserving trust.

The Escalation Playbook for Leaders is not a manual of authority; it is a manifesto for accountability. It shows how leaders can build mechanisms that encourage transparency, set clear thresholds for intervention, and empower teams to raise concerns without fear. True leadership is not in solving every problem personally, but in creating an ecosystem where problems surface early, and resolution is shared.

We also learned that escalation, when modelled correctly by leadership, sets the tone for culture. It signals that silence is not loyalty, and that transparency is not rebellion. It teaches teams that respect and honesty can coexist, that truth spoken with care strengthens rather than threatens collaboration.

Leadership maturity lies in knowing when to step in, when to step back, and when to let the system self-correct. This balance turns escalation into a lever of growth rather than a symptom of dysfunction.

"A culture where people fear escalation is a culture where leaders have already failed."

In the next chapter, we step away from frameworks and enter the *field* — into stories drawn from real corridors of corporate life. These stories, layered with human complexity and moral reflection, reveal what the theories of escalation look like when tested by emotion, power, and consequence.

"Leaders who embrace escalation build cultures of trust." – Corporate Truth

---

CHAPTER 14
STORIES FROM THE TRENCHES

"History doesn't repeat itself, but it often rhymes." – Mark Twain

Real-world stories illustrate escalation's power. From project conflicts to cultural clashes, stories reveal that escalation can either save or sink outcomes.

"History doesn't repeat itself in corporate corridors, but it rhymes — with escalations, crises, and silences that make-or-break careers."

Escalation theory is neat on paper. But in practice, it is messy, human, and unpredictable. This chapter collects stories from the trenches — anonymized but drawn from real-world corporate battles, to illustrate how escalation plays out in boardrooms, emails, and even silence.

Story: The Deadline That Became a Domino

At a global technology firm, a program manager escalated a missed dependency from a vendor. The escalation was sharp, factual, but copied the entire executive team.

- **What worked:** The vendor scrambled, delivered within 48 hours, and the project crossed the line.
- **What failed:** The public nature of the escalation strained the vendor relationship. Trust eroded, and future negotiations became costlier.

Lesson: Escalation solved the immediate issue but sowed long-term friction. A private escalation first could have balanced speed with relationship preservation.

Story: The Silent Sales Director

A regional sales director noticed a pricing error in a key bid but chose silence, fearing escalation would embarrass a senior executive who approved it. The error was exposed later by the client, costing millions in lost credibility.

- **What worked:** Silence avoided immediate embarrassment.
- **What failed:** The silence created reputational and financial damage far worse than a timely escalation would have.

Lesson: Silence in anger or fear may feel safe, but silence in duty is dangerous.

Story: The Escalation That Saved a Career

A young analyst escalated a data breach risk in a financial institution. He bypassed his manager and went directly to compliance leadership. The manager was furious, but weeks later, an external audit validated the analyst's warning.

- **What worked:** Courage and facts protected the firm.
- **What failed:** Chain-of-command friction damaged trust with the immediate manager.

Lesson: Sometimes escalation is worth personal risk — but escalation etiquette matters just as much as escalation courage.

Story: The Product Launch Meltdown

Context:
A multinational tech company was preparing for a high-stakes product launch. Engineering, Marketing, and Sales were at odds over timelines. Marketing had already pre-booked campaigns worth millions, while Engineering insisted the product wasn't ready.

Escalation:
The Engineering VP drafted a fiery escalation email blaming Marketing for "reckless commitments." Marketing shot back with their own escalation, accusing Engineering of "deliberate sandbagging." The CEO got dragged in. Meetings turned hostile.

What Failed:

- Escalation was driven by *frustration*, not *facts.*
- Leaders escalated *around each other*, bypassing direct resolution.
- Emails were weaponized, not tools of alignment.

Resolution:
The CEO halted all escalations and forced a 48-hour cooling-off period. A cross-functional "war room" was created with neutral facilitators. The product launch was delayed by 3 months but executed flawlessly.

Lesson Learned:
Escalations in anger are explosions. Escalations in silence, with documentation and structured facts, build credibility.

The Dotted-Line Dilemma

Context:
A regional manager in Asia reported directly to the Global Sales Director but also had a dotted line to the Country Head. Both leaders had conflicting priorities: one pushing global standardization, the other pushing local customization.

Escalation:
The regional manager felt trapped. Any escalation risked alienating one leader. Instead of firing off a complaint, she meticulously documented overlaps, impact on revenue, and presented it as a *business case* for alignment.

What Worked:

- She escalated *up*, not *around.*
- Data-driven, not emotional, framing.
- She asked for a *decision-making framework* rather than pointing fingers.

Resolution:
The Global Director and Country Head agreed on a hybrid strategy. The regional manager gained credibility as a "problem solver" rather than a "troublemaker."

Lesson Learned:
Escalation is not always about "sounding the alarm." It can be about "forcing clarity" at the leadership level.

Story: The Vendor Stand-off

Context:
A financial services company discovered major billing discrepancies with a critical vendor. The Operations team flagged the issue, but Procurement hesitated to escalate because the vendor relationship was politically sensitive.

Escalation:
The Operations manager drafted a sharp escalation to the CFO, attaching all invoice discrepancies. The CFO replied with a single line: *"Noted, but why was this not raised earlier?"*

The sting of the question forced the Operations manager to reflect. He realized his own delay weakened the escalation.

Resolution:
A calmer, revised escalation was sent, framed as:

- Facts of the discrepancy
- Financial risk if not corrected
- Request for leadership intervention with the vendor

The CFO supported the revised escalation and negotiated a settlement saving millions.

Lesson Learned:
Timing matters. Escalating too late can shift blame back at you. Silence at the wrong time costs credibility; silence at the right time prevents missteps.

Story: The Case of the "Angry Email"

Context:
In a consulting firm, a young manager felt disrespected by a senior partner who dismissed his ideas in a meeting. He drafted an emotional email at 11 PM, escalating directly to the partner's boss.

Escalation:
He pressed "send."

What Failed:

- Emotion overshadowed facts.
- The escalation was *personal*, not *professional.*
- The partner retaliated by questioning the manager's maturity.

Resolution:
HR intervened. The manager later admitted that had he waited a day, written a structured escalation citing project risks (rather than bruised ego), he would have gained support.

Lesson Learned:
Escalation is permanent once written; anger is temporary. The Bhagavad Gita reminds us that silence taken in a moment of anger is not weakness but wisdom — a pause that prevents words from becoming irreversible mistakes.".

Story: Silence That Won

Context:
In a European energy firm, a project director was being undermined by a peer in steering committee meetings. Every presentation was nitpicked, every proposal delayed. The director's team wanted him to escalate aggressively.

Escalation Choice:
Instead, he stayed silent during provocations, but maintained impeccable documentation. After three months, when the peer made a false claim in front of the CFO, the director calmly presented a binder of records.

Resolution:
The peer lost credibility overnight. The director emerged respected for his patience and preparedness.

Lesson Learned:
Silence at the right time is not weakness. It is positioning. Sometimes, the best escalation is letting the other person over-escalate themselves into disrepute.

Escalation is not just about speaking up — it is about speaking up **wisely**. As the ancient Hindu scripture Gita reminds us, unchecked anger leads to delusion, delusion to destruction. True mastery of escalation lies not just in knowing *when to act* but also *when to hold silence.*

"He who controls his speech at the time of anger saves both his dignity and his cause."

Across these stories, certain patterns emerge that are worth remembering:

- **Silence is not weakness** — it can be the most powerful escalation tool when timed well.
- **Documentation builds credibility** — facts carry more weight than emotions when things reach the top.
- **Escalation is a duty, not an ego trip** — framing it around the collective mission makes it palatable to leaders.
- **Patience protects reputations** — waiting to act until you have clarity often changes outcomes.
- **Tone defines trajectory** — an accusatory word can ignite fire, a measured one can open doors.
- **Escalation is not the end — it is a transition** — often the beginning of resolution, not the end of conflict.

> ***"Stories teach what strategies cannot." – Anonymous***

Looking Ahead

The stories in this chapter remind us that escalation is not a corporate process, it is a human condition. It unfolds in quiet conference rooms, tense email threads, and boardrooms where silence speaks louder than truth. Each narrative carried a moral heartbeat — showing that what often begins as a workplace dilemma is, at its core, a test of character.

From the manager who chose restraint over retaliation to the leader who found courage in transparency, every story reflected a different dimension of judgment under pressure. Some escalations ended in resolution; others left scars. But in each case, growth came not from victory, but from reflection.

As we close the trenches of today's corporate battles, a new battlefield awaits — one shaped not just by boardrooms and human egos, but by **algorithms, digital platforms, and artificial intelligence**.

Escalation tomorrow may not just mean sending an email to your boss. It may mean interacting with an AI system, filing a digital grievance in a global workflow, or questioning the ethics of automation decisions. The future of escalation will test not only our corporate maturity but also our ability to balance **speed, ethics, and humanity** in a world where machines play as big a role as managers.

As we step into the final chapter, we look ahead to a new frontier — a world where human judgment meets artificial intelligence, where ethics and algorithms intertwine, and where the very act of escalation is being redefined. The next chapter explores that uncertain yet promising terrain — the *future of escalation.* And so we step into our next chapter, **The Future of Escalation — AI, Ethics, and Beyond**

Chapter 15
The Future of Escalation — AI, Ethics, and Beyond

"The future depends on what you do today." – Mahatma Gandhi

The future of escalation will test how humans and machines interact. AI may surface risks faster than humans, but ethical choices will still rest with leaders. Escalation in this age is about balancing speed, ethics, and humanity.

As we stand at the intersection of technology, ethics, and human judgment, it's important to acknowledge that there is no definitive playbook for escalation in this evolving world. Artificial intelligence, algorithmic decisions, and digital communication have rewritten the rules faster than organizations can codify them. What worked yesterday may not hold tomorrow.

I do not claim expertise in predicting where this journey will lead, only the conviction that *experience itself* will become our greatest teacher. As professionals, we are collectively learning to navigate new moral frontiers — when to intervene, when to trust systems, and when to question them. The answers will not come from policies alone, but from the **judgment, empathy, and responsibility** we exercise as humans in an increasingly automated landscape.

The future of escalation will not be about creating rigid hierarchies or predefined steps but about nurturing **adaptive wisdom** — the ability to pause, assess, and act with integrity, no matter how advanced our tools become.

The art of escalation is entering uncharted territory. The battleground is no longer limited to boardrooms, email trails, or whispered corridor conversations. Today, escalation moves across **cloud platforms, digital ecosystems, and AI-powered decision-making systems**.

We are stepping into a future where escalation will be less about raising a voice and more about raising a flag in systems that are automated, decentralized, and sometimes beyond the comprehension of a single individual. This transformation demands a new mindset: escalation in the age of **machines, speed, and ethics.**

---

1. AI as the First Responder — and Gatekeeper

In many corporations, AI is already filtering complaints, routing escalation requests, and prioritizing tickets. Algorithms decide whether an employee grievance is "urgent" or whether a customer escalation gets flagged for human review.

This raises critical questions: *What if the algorithm is biased?* What if an escalation never reaches the right leader because the system incorrectly classified it as "low impact"?

The future will demand a dual escalation: **one about the issue itself, and another about how the system handled it.** Escalating *the escalation system* will become a reality. Leaders must therefore treat algorithms not as neutral arbiters, but as entities requiring oversight, transparency, and ethical accountability.

---

2. The Speed Paradox: Instant Escalations, Lasting Consequences

In a hyper-connected workplace, escalation is instantaneous. A frustrated Slack message, a viral tweet from an employee, or a whistleblower post on LinkedIn can reach global leaders before traditional hierarchies even react.

But speed comes with danger. Escalations made in haste, without full facts, can damage reputations, trigger regulatory scrutiny, and even collapse partnerships. In the digital future, the **half-life of silence shrinks, but the shelf-life of escalation grows longer**. What you escalate online, stays online.

The challenge for tomorrow's leaders will be to balance urgency with deliberation, ensuring escalation is not just fast, but also fair and accurate.

---

3. Escalating Machines: When Technology Itself Fails

Imagine a global payroll AI glitch leaving thousands unpaid. Or an autonomous trading bot triggering billion-dollar losses. In such cases, escalation isn't about people misbehaving, it's about **systems misfiring.**

The future escalation playbook must therefore include **machine failure protocols**: who gets alerted when an AI system goes wrong, who decides when to shut it down, and how accountability is traced in the absence of human intent.

This introduces a new ethical dilemma: *can we escalate "responsibility" when the decision-maker was a machine?*

---

4. The Ethical Dimension: Escalating What Machines Miss

AI systems are powerful, but they are not moral. They optimize for efficiency, not fairness, for probability, not empathy. In this vacuum, escalation becomes a moral act.

- An employee might escalate that an algorithm is rejecting women candidates disproportionately.
- A manager might escalate that an AI performance tool is unfairly downgrading employees from certain regions.
- A whistleblower might point out that customer data is being used in ways the public never consented to.

Here, escalation is not about workflow but about **ethics**. And those who escalate may well be safeguarding the corporate soul.

The *Bhagavad Gita* reminds us: *"When dharma declines, it is the duty of the wise to act."* In the digital age, dharma often means standing up against invisible, coded injustices.

---

5. The Rise of Collective Escalations

Another emerging trend is the rise of **collective escalations**. Employees on platforms like Blind, Glassdoor, or LinkedIn can unite and escalate concerns — not to a single manager, but to the entire world. Investors, regulators, and customers now form part of the escalation audience.

This democratization of escalation strips leaders of their monopoly over narratives. Tomorrow's leaders must master not just **internal escalation management**, but also **external escalation diplomacy.**

---

6. Preparing for the Future: The Escalation 2030 Playbook

Looking ahead, escalation will be reshaped by three imperatives:

- **Transparency:** Every escalation, whether routed through AI or humans, must be traceable, explainable, and auditable.
- **Ethical Courage:** Leaders will be judged less on how they resolve operational escalations and more on how they handle ethical ones.
- **Digital Diplomacy:** Escalation management will extend beyond corporate walls into media, regulators, and society. Leaders must learn to respond with speed, empathy, and credibility in a digital spotlight.

Closing Reflection

The future of escalation is both exciting and unsettling. Machines will act as gatekeepers, employees will wield digital megaphones, and ethical escalations will often define legacies.

Escalation, once a tactical skill, is fast becoming a **strategic leadership capability.** Those who master it will not just navigate conflicts, they will shape the trust, ethics, and resilience of their organizations.

"Our tools shape us, but our choices define us."
In the end, the future of escalation will not just be determined by algorithms or platforms. It will also be determined by leaders who choose clarity over confusion, ethics over expediency, and courage over silence.

Machines may process data, but only humans can escalate with conscience. The algorithms of the future will continue to refine judgment, yet it is empathy that must remain the operating system of leadership. As we navigate this uncharted era of AI, automation, and ethics, escalation will no longer be about protocol, it will be about presence. The courage to pause, question, and act with awareness may become our most enduring leadership code.

"The future of escalation is human judgment amplified, not replaced, by machines." – Anonymous

CHAPTER 16

WHAT WE'VE LEARNED — THE DISCIPLINE BEHIND COURAGE

"Clarity without structure is chaos; structure without empathy is bureaucracy. The art lies in blending both." — Anonymous

Bringing Structure to Judgment

By now, we've seen escalation in its many forms — boardroom battles, quiet hesitations, and moments of ethical clarity. What separates instinct from leadership is discipline, the ability to act with both structure and sensitivity. What emerges is a simple truth. escalation is not a single act; it's a framework for clarity, courage, and constructive communication.

The CFIA and CIAE+ frameworks, first introduced earlier, now return as mirrors of that discipline, guiding how we clarify, communicate, and choose courage when it counts. They serve not as rigid checklists, but as decision compasses for professionals navigating when, how, and why to escalate.

Two companion frameworks, the **CFIA Model** and the **CIAE+ Formula** — help professionals do both. They are not sequential steps, but **interchangeable lenses**: you can look at any escalation through either, depending on whether you are clarifying your message or framing a decision.

Early in the book, CIAE was introduced as the structural framework for communicating escalation.

At that stage, the leadership journey was still anchored in clarity and fact.
CIAE helped ensure communication was clean, non-emotional, and rooted in objectivity.

CIAE established a baseline of communication maturity — ensuring that escalation travelled with clarity and without accusation.

But as leaders progress, communication must carry more than facts.

It must carry **humanity**.

And that is why the framework evolves.

The Evolution to CIAE+ — The Complete Communication Lens

Context · Impact · Ask · Evidence · Empathy

At the early stages of escalation maturity, Evidence is essential.
But at higher levels of leadership, Empathy becomes equally critical.

Empathy is not a compromise; it is a strategy. It diffuses resistance, acknowledges the realities others navigate, and makes room for genuine influence to emerge.

CIAE+ adds what great leaders intuitively practice:

Context — Explain without overwhelming.
Impact — Make consequences visible.
Ask — Guide the next step.
Evidence — Ground the truth.
Empathy — Honour the relationship.

When communication is factual without empathy, it can feel cold.
When it is empathetic without evidence, it becomes vague.

CIAE+ brings them together, a union of truth and tact. **Empathy doesn't dilute escalation — it dignifies it.** In a culture where words often outpace intentions, CIAE+ is the bridge that maintains professionalism and trust even in disagreement.

---

1. The CFIA Model — Clarify, Frame, Inform, Act

The **CFIA** model is designed for those moments when an issue seems complex, and emotions threaten to cloud logic.

It helps you bring method to your instinct.

Step	What It Means	Key Questions to Ask
Clarify	Understand the issue in its entirety before reacting.	What exactly happened? What are the facts? What is perception vs. evidence?
Frame	Structure the narrative to make it understandable and actionable.	How can I describe this issue objectively? What's the context?
Inform	Communicate the issue to the right audience, in the right tone.	Who needs to know, and what's the right medium — email, call, or meeting?
Act	Escalate or resolve based on readiness and impact.	Do I have enough clarity and buy-in to move forward?

Tip: Clarity comes before action. Many failed escalations stem from skipping the first two steps — clarity and framing.

2. The CIAE+ Formula — Context, Impact, Ask, Evidence, Empathy

If CFIA is about **how** to escalate, **CIAE+** is about **how to communicate**.
It's especially relevant when you're writing an escalation email, presenting an issue to leadership, or even intervening in a heated conversation.

Step	What It Means	Application in Practice
Context	Set the background, not as a justification, but to ensure shared understanding.	"Over the past quarter, vendor invoices have consistently been delayed due to…"
Impact	Explain why this matters. Translate the issue into business, customer, or compliance impact.	"This could delay Q3 reporting and affect audit readiness."
Ask	Clearly state what you need from the receiver.	"Request leadership support to align finance and operations timelines."
Evidence	Supporting facts, data, or documentation that substantiate the issue and remove ambiguity.	"Attached is the invoice log and the email trail highlighting the delays for your reference."
Empathy	Acknowledge pressures or constraints of others.	"I recognize the team has competing priorities, but aligning early will help avoid last-minute escalations."

When Both Models Intersect

Interchangeable Wisdom — Choosing the Lens

In practice, the best leaders move fluidly between **CFIA and CIAE+**:

- When communication clarity is the priority, **CFIA** offers structure.
- When decision framing or influence is at stake, **CIAE+** provides guidance.

Neither is superior; both are situational.
Used together, they create a rhythm of **clarity → communication → resolution** — the very essence of escalation mastery.

When you combine **CFIA** and **CIAE+**, escalation becomes both **structured** and **humane**.

- CFIA gives you the *clarity to act.*
- CIAE+ gives you the *language to connect.*

Together, they create a **360° framework** of corporate escalation — grounded in logic, guided by empathy.

Example:
A project manager facing repeated missed deliverables first used CFIA to clarify the scope of the issue and frame supporting data. Then, using CIAE+, she wrote to her regional lead — giving context, quantifying the impact, making a clear ask, and showing empathy for bandwidth challenges.

The issue was resolved in one meeting — not because it was small, but because it was structured.

The Takeaway

Escalation is not a reaction, it's a craft.
The **CFIA** and **CIAE+** frameworks are not corporate theories; they are reminders that:

- **Facts deserve framing**,
- **Actions demand empathy**, and
- **Courage needs structure**.

As you apply these models, remember that they are not meant to *replace judgment*, but to *refine it.*
Because at the end of every escalation lies a leader deciding whether to react — or rise.

"The wise escalate not to be heard louder, but to make clarity visible."

The Evolution of CIAE — From Evidence to Empathy

"As leadership deepens, so does the way we make sense of problems."

When the **CIAE framework** first appeared in *Chapter 4*, the final "E" represented **Evidence** — a signal that facts and documentation are the foundation of credibility. That interpretation remains valuable; **evidence anchors trust.**

But as the story of this book, and of corporate leadership itself unfolded, the framework matured.
We came to see that while **Evidence** strengthens the argument, **Empathy** strengthens the relationship. And in a world where influence travels faster than instruction, connection often determines whether action follows.

Thus, CIAE matured into CIAE+ — where Evidence and Empathy stand together not as a correction, but as a completion of the communication lens.
Evidence convinces the mind; empathy moves the heart. Together, they turn escalation into partnership.

This evolution mirrors the book's central message: that effective escalation is not about winning a point but about **earning trust while driving progress.**

EPILOGUE

ESCALATE TO ELEVATE

"Great leaders don't avoid conflict, they navigate it." – Anonymous

Escalation is not about ego, it's about action. Great leaders don't avoid escalations, they channel them. Escalation, when done with wisdom and balance, elevates both people and organizations. *We also draw strength from timeless philosophy. In the Hindu scripture The Bhagavad Gita (Chapter 2, Verse 63), Lord Krishna explains:*

'From anger, delusion arises; from delusion, bewilderment of memory; when memory is bewildered, intelligence is lost; and when intelligence is lost, one falls down."

In other words: anger clouds judgment. Silence at the heat of the moment is not passivity, but the highest form of escalation control. The Bhagavad Gita reminds us: restraint in anger leads to wiser action.

"Escalation is duty-bound courage, not reckless noise."

SOURCES/REFERENCES

This book is a blend of lived experience, leadership reflection, and curated wisdom. While the core frameworks and narratives emerge from over two decades of professional practice across corporate governance, finance, and organizational leadership, select references from management literature, psychology, and philosophy have been integrated to provide context, depth, and balance.

All real-life examples and case studies have been **anonymized** and **generalized** to preserve confidentiality while retaining their instructive value. Where cited, published works and thought frameworks have been acknowledged in the section that follows.

1. Covey, Stephen R. *The 7 Habits of Highly Effective People.* Free Press, 1989.
   (Referenced for concepts of proactive leadership, responsibility, and influence.

2. Drucker, Peter F. *The Effective Executive.* HarperCollins, 1966.
   (Referenced for principles of decision-making, delegation, and leadership accountability.)

3. Carnegie, Dale. *How to Win Friends and Influence People.* Simon & Schuster, 1936.
   (Referenced for tone and relationship management in upward communication.)

4. Schein, Edgar H. *Organizational Culture and Leadership.* Jossey-Bass, 2010.
(Referenced for understanding culture-driven escalation behaviors.)

5. Goleman, Daniel. *Emotional Intelligence: Why It Can Matter More Than IQ.* Bantam Books, 1995. *(Referenced for emotional regulation and self-awareness in escalation psychology.)*

6. Hofstede's Cultural Dimensions and Erin Meyer's Framework: The Culture Map

   (Referenced for Cultural Dimensions of Escalation)

7. *SCARF Model, David Rock*

   (Referenced for Neuroscience & the Threat Response while escalating)

8. Global publications featuring studies on conflict resolution and decision velocity.

9. *Verses from The Bhagavad Gita (Hindu Scripture)*

10. *Public articles on AI ethics, data-driven decision-making, and algorithmic accountability.*
